ੴ

SIKH BABY NAMES

(1200 selected and meaningful names for boys & girls)

COMPILED AND EDITED BY :

MANDEEP KAUR DIMPY

ਸਿਖ ਬਚਿਆਂ ਦੇ ਨਾਂ

ਸੰਧਾਦਕ :

ਮਨਦੀਧ ਕੇਰ ਡਿਮਪੀ

Dimpy, Mandeep Kaur (Ed.)
SIKH BACHIAN DE NAA
(Sikh Baby Names)
New Delhi, Star : 2003 (Reprint)
ISBN : 81-86264-04-3

First Edition- 1994
Second Edition-1999
Third Edition- 2003
Fourth Edition- 2009

Price : (In India) Rs. 100
(In U.K.) £ 4.95

Publishers :
STAR PUBLICATIONS (PVT.) LTD.
4/5, Asaf Ali Road,
New Delhi-110 002 (India)

Distributors in UK :
STAR PUBLISHERS' DISTRIBUTORS
55, Warren Street, London W1T 5NW (U.K.)

TYPESETTING & PRINTED BY : PULLSHOPPE, NEW DELHI-110 002

To
Long life and happiness
of the
Newly-born babies !

ੴ

ੴ

ABOUT THIS BOOK :

This glossary of names has been especially prepared for the Sikh-children, but non-Sikh parents can also benefit from it, because of the common roots of the words which have been compiled here.

Most of the names of the people of Indian born religions come from Sanskrit origin, but they take somewhat different shapes and pronunciations in different regions. Each region and community in a vast country like India has its own peculiar accent and habits in pronouncing words, which are otherwise common in many languages. A Bengali would always say 'Bidhan' instead of 'Vidhan' as pronounced in Sanskrit or Sanskritised Hindi.

Punjabi language has its very close relationship with Sanskrit, but it has mostly adopted 'Prakrit' pronunciation instead of 'Sanskrit'. Therefore 'Virendra.' (वीरेन्द्र, ਵੀਰੇਂਦ੍ਰ) is always prnounced as Virender (वीरेन्दर, ਵੀਰੇਂਦਰ). Similarly

'Rajendra' becomes 'Rajinder', 'Prabhu' becomes 'Prabh', 'Bhanu' is pronounced as 'Bhan' etc. While preparing this glossary, the Punjabi accent has been kept in mind.

In Sikh names there is hardly any difference in male or female names. The difference appears only when suffix 'Singh' (for males) and 'Kaur' (for females) is added with the first name. But in some Sikh families now, there is a trend of using only first name like Aparna, Anita, Nilima, and then is added suffix 'Kaur', (Aparna Kaur), 'Singh' (Anita Singh) or caste/surname (like Nilima Kohli). In many cases by adding 'a' to a name it becomes female name; as Amit-Amita, Susheel-Susheela, Saral-Sarla etc.

I have tried to make this glossary as comprehensive as possible. Any suggestions, however, in this regard will be most welcome.

—Editor.

ੴ

ਸੰਪਾਦਕ ਵਲੋਂ

ਇਹ ਕੋਸ਼ ਖਾਸ ਤੌਰ ਤੇ ਸਿਖ ਬਚਿਆਂ ਲਈ ਤਿਆਰ ਕੀਤਾ ਗਿਆ ਹੈ, ਪਰ ਗੈਰਸਿਖ ਮਾਂ-ਪਿਉ ਵੀ ਇਸ ਤੋਂ ਪੂਰਾ ਲਾਭ ਲੈ ਸਕਦੇ ਹਨ, ਕਿਉਂਕਿ ਜਿਹੜੇ ਲਫ਼ਜ਼ ਇੱਥੇ ਇਕੱਤਰ ਕੀਤੇ ਗਏ ਹਨ ਉਹਨਾਂ ਦਾ ਸੋਮਾ ਤਾਂ ਸਭ ਲਈ ਸਮਾਨ ਹੈ।

ਭਾਰਤ ਵਿਚ ਜਨਮੇ ਧਰਮਾਂ ਨੂੰ ਮੰਨਣ ਵਾਲੇ ਲੋਕਾਂ ਦੇ ਬਹੁਤੇ ਨਾਮ ਸੰਸਕ੍ਰਿਤ ਮੂਲ ਤੋਂ ਉਪਜੇ ਹੁੰਦੇ ਹਨ, ਪਰ ਵਖਰੇ-ਵਖਰੇ ਖੇਤਰਾਂ ਅਤੇ ਧਾਰਮਿਕ-ਸਮਾਜਿਕ ਮਾਹੌਲ ਵਿਚ ਉਹਨਾਂ ਦਾ ਰੂਪ ਤੇ ਉੱਚਾਰਣ ਕੁਝ ਵਖਰਾ ਹੋ ਜਾਂਦਾ ਹੈ। ਭਾਰਤ ਜਿਹੇ ਵਿਸ਼ਾਲ ਦੇਸ਼ ਵਿਚ ਵਖਰੇ-ਵਖਰੇ ਇਲਾਕਿਆਂ ਤੇ ਕੌਮਾਂ ਵਿਚ ਸ਼ਬਦਾਂ ਨੂੰ ਬੋਲਣ ਦੇ ਆਪਣੇ ਵਿਸ਼ੇਸ਼ ਢੰਗ ਤੇ ਸੁਰ ਹਨ, ਭਾਵੇਂ ਇਹ ਸ਼ਬਦ ਬਹੁਤੀਆਂ ਭਾਸ਼ਾਂਵਾਂ ਵਿਚ ਮੂਲ ਰੂਪ ਵਿਚ ਸਮਾਨ ਹੁੰਦੇ ਹਨ, ਸੰਸਕ੍ਰਿਤ ਜਾਂ ਤਤਸਮ ਹਿੰਦੀ ਵਿਚ ਬੋਲੇ ਜਾਣ ਵਾਲੇ ਸ਼ਬਦ 'ਵਿਧਾਨ' ਨੂੰ ਇਕ ਬੰਗਾਲੀ 'ਬਿਧਾਨ' ਹੀ ਬੋਲੇਗਾ।

ਪੰਜਾਬੀ ਦਾ ਸੰਸਕ੍ਰਿਤ ਦੇ ਨਾਲ ਬੜਾ ਨੇੜੇ ਦਾ ਸੰਬੰਧ ਹੈ, ਪਰ ਉਸਦੀ ਉੱਚਾਰਣ ਦੀ ਰੀਤੀ ਸੰਸਕ੍ਰਿਤ ਦੀ ਬਜਾਏ 'ਪ੍ਰਾਕ੍ਰਿਤ' ਦੇ ਅਨੁਸਾਰ ਹੈ। ਇਹੋ ਕਾਰਨ ਹੈ ਕਿ 'ਵੀਰੇਂਦ੍ਰ' ਨੂੰ ਪੰਜਾਬੀ ਵਿਚ ਵੀਰੇਂਦਰ ਬੋਲਿਆ ਤੇ ਲਿਖਿਆ ਜਾਂਦਾ ਹੈ। ਇਸੇ ਤਰ੍ਹਾਂ 'ਗਜੇਂਦ੍ਰ' 'ਰਾਜਿੰਦਰ', 'ਪ੍ਰਭੁ', 'ਪ੍ਰਭ' ਅਤੇ 'ਭਾਨੁ' 'ਭਾਨ' ਬਣ ਜਾਂਦਾ ਹੈ।

ਇਹ ਕੋਸ਼ ਤਿਆਰ ਕਰਣ ਵੇਲੇ ਪੰਜਾਬੀ ਸੁਭਾ ਨੂੰ ਧਿਆਨ ਵਿਚ ਰਖਿਆ ਗਿਆ ਹੈ।

ੴ

ਸਿਖ ਬੱਚਿਆਂ ਦੇ ਨਾਵਾਂ ਵਿਚ ਮੁੰਡੇ ਜਾਂ ਕੁੜੀ ਦੇ ਨਾਂ ਵਿਚ ਕੋਈ ਖਾਸ ਫਰਕ ਨਹੀਂ ਹੁੰਦਾ। ਫਰਕ ਪਿਛੇਤਰ ਲੱਗੇ 'ਸਿੰਘ' ਜਾਂ 'ਕੌਰ' ਤੋਂ ਹੀ ਪਤਾ ਲਗਦਾ ਹੈ। ਪਰ ਹੁਣ ਕੁਝਕੁ ਸਿਖ ਪਰਿਵਾਰਾਂ ਵਿਚ ਇਹ ਰੁਝਾਨ ਬਣਿਆ ਹੈ ਕਿ ਉਹ ਕੁੜੀਆਂ ਦੇ ਨਾਂ ਆਮ ਕੁੜੀਆਂ ਦੇ ਨਾਂਵਾਂ ਜਿਹੇ ਰੱਖਣ ਲਗ ਪਏ ਹਨ। ਜਿਵੇਂ ਅਪਰਨਾ, ਅਨੀਤਾ, ਨੀਲਿਮਾ ਤੇ ਉਸ ਨਾਲ ਪਿਛੇਤਰ ਕੌਰ (ਅਪਰਨਾ ਕੌਰ) ਜਾਂ 'ਸਿੰਘ' (ਅਨੀਤਾ ਸਿੰਘ) ਲਗਾਉਂਦੇ ਹਨ ਜਾਂ ਜਾਤਸੂਚਕ ਪਿਛੇਤਰ ਦੀ ਵਰਤੋਂ ਕਰਦੇ ਹਨ ਜਿਵੇਂ ਨੀਲਮ ਕੋਹਲੀ ਆਮ ਤੌਰ ਤੇ ਜੇ ਕਿਸੇ ਸ਼ਬਦ ਦੇ ਨਾਲ 'ਅ' ਜੋੜ ਦਿੱਤਾ ਜਾਏ ਤਾਂ ਉਹ ਇਸਤਰੀਵਾਚਕ ਬਣ ਜਾਂਦਾ ਹੈ ਜਿਵੇਂ ਅਮਿਤ-ਅਮਿਤਾ, ਸੁਸ਼ੀਲ-ਸੁਸ਼ੀਲਾ, ਸਰਲ-ਸਰਲਾ ਆਦਿ।

ਮੈਂ ਇਸ ਕੋਸ਼ ਨੂੰ ਜਿਥੇ ਤੀਕ ਸੰਭਵ ਸੀ, ਵਿਆਪਕ ਬਣਾਉਣ ਦਾ ਯਤਨ ਕੀਤਾ ਹੈ। ਇਸ ਬਾਰੇ ਉਸਾਰੂ ਸੁਝਾਵਾਂ ਦਾ ਸਦਾ ਸੁਆਗਤ ਕੀਤਾ ਜਾਏਗਾ।

ਮਨਦੀਪ ਕੌਰ ਛਿੰਪੀ

ੴ

A ਅ

Aakash ਆਕਾਸ਼ Sky

Aakaar ਆਕਾਰ Shape

Abhishek ਅਭਿਸ਼ੇਕ Anointing

Abhilasha ਅਭਿਲਾਸ਼ਾ Desire

Abhinav ਅਭਿਨਵ Novel

Abhai ਅਭੈ Without fear

Abhijeet ਅਭਿਜੀਤ Victorious

Abhiroop ਅਭਿਰੂਪ Pleasing

Achal ਅਚਲ Constant, Mountain

Achint ਅਚਿੰਤ Without worry

Adeeb ਅਦੀਬ Writer

Adesh ਆਦੇਸ਼ Command

Adarsh ਆਦਰਸ਼ Ideal

Adarshpreet ਆਦਰਸ਼ਪ੍ਰੀਤ Love of Ideals

Adarshpal ਆਦਰਸ਼ਪਾਲ Fosterer of Ideals

ੴ

Adishwar	ਆਦੀਸ਼ਵਰ	The first God
Agam	ਅਗਮ	Inaccessible, God
Agamjit	ਅਗਮਜੀਤ	Victory of God
Agampreet	ਅਗਮਪੀਤ	Love for God
Ajeet	ਅਜੀਤ	Invincible
Ajai	ਅਜੈ-ਅਜਯ	Invincible
Ajeetpal	ਅਜੀਤਪਾਲ	Invincible Fosterer
Ajaipal	ਅਜੈਪਾਲ	Invincible Fosterer
Ajaipreet	ਅਜੈਪ੍ਰੀਤ	Invincible Love
Ajitabh	ਅਜਿਤਾਭ	Imconquered Glow
Ajitesh	ਅਜਿਤੇਸ਼	Invincible God
Akashdeep	ਅਕਾਸ਼ਦੀਪ	Sky lamp
Akhand	ਅਖੰਡ	Undivided
Akhil	ਅਖਿਲ	All
Akhiljeet	ਅਖਿਲਜੀਤ	All victorious
Akhilpal	ਅਖਿਲਪਾਲ	Fosterer of All
Akhilpreet	ਅਖਿਲਪ੍ਰੀਤ	Love for all
Akal	ਅਕਾਲ	Ageless, Supreme being, God

ੴ

Akaljeet	ਅਕਾਲਜੀਤ	Victory of God
Akalpreet	ਅਕਾਲਪ੍ਰੀਤ	Love of God
Alok	ਆਲੋਕ	Light
Amrit	ਅਮ੍ਰਿਤ	Nector
Amritpal	ਅੰਮ੍ਰਿਤਪਾਲ	Preserver of Nectar
Amar	ਅਮਰ	Immortal
Amarjeet	ਅਮਰਜੀਤ	Immortal Victory
Amardeep	ਅਮਰਦੀਪ	Immortal Lamp
Amandeep	ਅਮਨਦੀਪ	Light of Peace
Aman	ਅਮਨ	Peace
Amanpreet	ਅਮਨਪ੍ਰੀਤ	Love of peace
Amit	ਅਮਿਤ	Without limit
Amitoj	ਅਮਿਤੋਜ	Unlimited Glow
Amarpal	ਅਮਰਪਾਲ	Immortal Protector
Amarjot	ਅਮਰਜੋਤ	Immortal flame
Amarinder	ਅਮਰਿੰਦਰ	Immortal King
Amitesh	ਅਮਿਤੇਸ਼	Limitless God
Amrik	ਅਮਰੀਕ	God of sky

ੴ

Ambreesh	ਅੰਬਰੀਸ਼	God of sky
Amanjeet	ਅਮਨਜੀਤ	Victory for peace
Amal	ਅਮਲ	Pure
Amalinder	ਅਮਲਿੰਦਰ	Pure God
Amolak	ਅਮੋਲਕ	Priceless
Amitabh	ਅਮਿਤਾਭ	Unlimited brilliance, Lord Buddha
Anmol	ਅਨਮੋਲ	Priceless
Anupreet	ਅਨੂਪ੍ਰੀਤ	With Love
Angad	ਅੰਗਦ	Anornament, Name of Second Sikh Guru
Anurag	ਅਨੂਰਾਗ	Love
Anang	ਅਨੰਗ	Cupid—God of love, Kamdev
Anangpal	ਅਨੰਗਪਾਲ	Protector of cupid
Anangjeet	ਅਨੰਗਜੀਤ	One who conquers cupid, Shiva
Anadi	ਅਨਾਦਿ	Eternal
Anirudh	ਅਨਿਰੁੱਧ	Free
Anil	ਅਨਿਲ	Air

ੴ

Aneel	ਅਨੀਲ	White
Aneesh	ਅਨੀਸ਼	Supreme
Anuj	ਅਨੁਜ	Younger Brother
Anujpreet	ਅਨੁਜਪ੍ਰੀਤ	Love for younger brother
Anujpal	ਅਨੁਜਪਾਲ	Fosterer of younger brother
Anupam	ਅਨੁਪਮ	Matchless
Antar	ਅੰਤਰ	Heart, Inner
Antardhyan	ਅੰਤਰਧਿਆਨ	Meditation
Antarjot	ਅੰਤਰਜੋਤ	Inner light
Anand	ਆਨੰਦ	Pleasure, Bliss
Anubhuti	ਅਨੁਭੂਤਿ	Feeling
Anubhav	ਅਨੁਭਵ	Experience
Anuranjan	ਅਨੁਰੰਜਨ	Pleasure, Affection
Anshuman	ਅੰਸ਼ੁਮਾਨ	Sun
Anant	ਅਨੰਤ	Endless
Anantjeet	ਅਨੰਤਜੀਤ	Endless Victory
Antarpreet	ਅੰਤਰਪ੍ਰੀਤ	Deep Love, Inner Love

ੴ

Anantpal	ਅਨੰਤਪਾਲ	Infinite Fosterer
Anantpreet	ਅਨੰਤਪ੍ਰੀਤ	Infinite Love
Anandsarup	ਆਨੰਦਸਰੂਪ	Blissful Form
Anandpal	ਆਨੰਦਪਾਲ	Fosterer of Bliss
Anoopjeet	ਅਨੂਪਜੀਤ	Victory for unique
Anurag	ਅਨੁਰਾਗ	Devotion, Love
Anoop	ਅਨੂਪ	Unique
Aparna	ਅਪਰਨਾ	Goddess Parvati
Aparajit	ਅਪਰਾਜਿਤ	Unconquered
Arijinder	ਅਰਿਜਿੰਦਰ	Destroyer of Enemy
Arshdeep	ਅਰਸ਼ਦੀਪ	Light of the sky
Arun	ਅਰੁਨ	Red, Dawn, Morning Sun
Arun Parkash	ਅਰੁਨਪ੍ਰਕਾਸ਼	Red Light, Light of the morning sun
Arundeep	ਅਰੁਨਦੀਪ	Red Lamp
Arunpreet	ਅਰੁਨਪ੍ਰੀਤ	Who loves redness, one who loves morning sun
Arvind	ਅਰਵਿੰਦ	Lotus
Arvinder	ਅਰਵਿੰਦਰ	God of Lotus

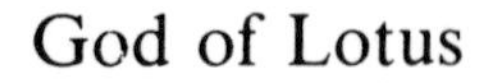

ੴ

Aridaman	ਅਰਿਦਮਨ	Destroyer of Enemy
Arjun, Arjan	ਅਰਜੁਨ	Bright, Name of fifth Sikh Guru, one of the Pandavas
Arpita	ਅਰਪਿਤਾ	Dedicated
Arth	ਅਰਥ	Meaning
Arthdeep	ਅਰਥਦੀਪ	Meaningfull lamp
Archan	ਅਰਚਨ	Worship
Arijeet	ਅਰਿਜੀਤ	Conquerer of Enemies.
Aseem	ਅਸੀਮ	Unlimited (M)
Aseema	ਅਸੀਮਾ	Unlimited (F)
Ashish	ਆਸ਼ੀਸ਼	Blessing
Ashu	ਆਸ਼ੂ	Full of hope, Quickly
Ashok	ਅਸ਼ੋਕ	Without grief
Asha	ਆਸ਼ਾ	Hope
Ashawant	ਆਸ਼ਾਵੰਤ	Hopeful
Ashutosh	ਆਸ਼ੁਤੋਸ਼	Easy to please, Lord Shiva
Atam	ਆਤਮ	Self
Atamjeet	ਆਤਮਜੀਤ	Victory over self
Atal	ਅਟਲ	Firm

ੴ

Atalvir	ਅਟੱਲਵੀਰ	Firm Brave
Atalbahadur	ਅਟੱਲਬਹਾਦਰ	Firm brave
Atul	ਅਤੁਲ	Inestimable, Matchless
Atulvir	ਅਤੁਲਵੀਰ	Unparalelled brave
Ati	ਅਤੀ	Very much, Supreme
Atinder	ਅਤਿੰਦਰ	Supreme God
Atinderjeet	ਅਤਿੰਦਰਜੀਤ	Victory of God
Atinderpal	ਅਤਿੰਦਰਪਾਲ	God Fosterer
Avneet	ਅਵਨੀਤ	Modest
Avtar	ਅਵਤਾਰ	Incarnation
Avinash	ਅਵਿਨਾਸ਼	Indestructible
Avani	ਅਵਨੀ	Earth
Avanipal	ਅਵਨੀਪਾਲ	King
Avanipreet	ਅਵਨੀਪ੍ਰੀਤ	Love of earth
Avanideep	ਅਵਨੀਦੀਤ	Lamp of earth
Avaninder	ਅਵਨਿੰਦਰ	Lord of Earth
Avaneesh	ਅਵਨੀਸ਼	Lord of Earth

ੴ

B ਬ

Baldeep	ਬਲਦੀਪ	Lamp of strength
Baldev	ਬਲਦੇਵ	Lord of strength
Baljinder	ਬਲਜਿੰਦਰ	Lord of strength
Baljit	ਬਲਜੀਤ	Victory of strength
Balawinder	ਬਲਵਿੰਦਰ	Lord of strength
Balpreet	ਬਲਪ੍ਰੀਤ	Love of strength
Balbir	ਬਲਬੀਰ	Brave
Bani	ਬਾਨੀ	Sayings of the Guru
Banita	ਬਨਿਤਾ	Lady
Basant	ਬਸੰਤ	Spring
Basantroop	ਬਸੰਤਰੂਪ	Shape of spring
Basantpreet	ਬਸੰਤਪ੍ਰੀਤ	Love of spring
Basantdeep	ਬਸੰਤਦੀਪ	Lamp of spring
Bahadur	ਬਹਾਦੁਰ	Brave
Bachan	ਬਚਨ	word, promise
Bachanpal	ਬਚਨਪਾਲ	Fosterer of Word, One who keeps promise

ੴ

Bachanpreet	ਬਚਨਪ੍ਰੀਤ	Love of word
Bachint	ਬਚਿੰਤ	Without worry
Barjinder	ਬਰਜਿੰਦਰ	Lord of strength
Balkar	ਬਲਕਾਰ	Full of strength
Baljiwan	ਬਲਜੀਵਨ	Life with strength
Baltej	ਬਲਤੇਜ	Glow of strength
Balpreet	ਬਲਪ੍ਰੀਤ	Love of strength
Balvan	ਬਲਵਾਨ	Strong
Beant	ਬੇਅੰਤ	Immeasurable, Endless
Beantpal	ਬੇਅੰਤਪਾਲ	Fosterer of immeasurable
Bhan/Bhanu	ਭਾਨ/ਭਾਨੂ	Sun
Bhanpreet	ਭਾਨਪ੍ਰੀਤ	Love of sun
Bhavdeep	ਭਵਦੀਪ	Lamp of the word
Bhavneet	ਭਵਨੀਤ	Moral of the world
Bhavleen	ਭਵਲੀਨ	Engrossed in the world
Bhushan	ਭੂਸ਼ਨ	Ornament
Bhavna	ਭਾਵਨਾ	Feeling
Bhagat	ਭਗਤ	Devotee

ੴ

Bhagatjeev	ਭਗਤਜੀਵ	Devoted life.
Bhagatpreet	ਭਗਤਪ੍ਰੀਤ	Love for devotee
Bhagwant	ਭਗਵੰਤ	God
Bhagwantjot	ਭਗਵੰਤਜੋਤ	Light of God
Bhagwantroop	ਭਗਵੰਤਰੂਪ	God form
Bhajan	ਭਜਨ	Devotional song
Bhajanjeet	ਭਜਨਜੀਤ	Victory of devotion
Bhajanpreet	ਭਜਨਪ੍ਰੀਤ	Love for devotion
Bharpur	ਭਰਪੂਰ	Full, Overflowing
Bhavan	ਭਾਵਨ	Pleasing, Attractive
Bhupal	ਭੂਪਾਲ	King
Bhupraj	ਭੂਪਰਾਜ	King of kings
Bhupesh	ਭੂਪੇਸ਼	God of kings
Bhupinder	ਭੂਪਿੰਦਰ	God of Kings
Bhupinderjeet	ਭੁਪਿੰਦਰਜੀਤ	Victory for supreme God
Bhupinderpal	ਭੁਪਿੰਦਰਪਾਲ	Preserved by God
Bikram	ਬਿਕਰਮ	Valour
Bikramjit	ਬਿਕਰਮਜੀਤ	Victory for valour

ੴ

Binwant	ਬਿਨਵੰਤ	Full of modesty
Bimal	ਬਿਮਲ	Pure
Bindu	ਬਿੰਦੂ	A drop, A dot
Bishan	ਬਿਸ਼ਨ	Pure God, Lord Vishnu
Bishanpreet	ਬਿਸ਼ਨਪ੍ਰੀਤ	Love for pure God
Bishanjeet	ਬਿਸ਼ਨਜੀਤ	Victory for pure God
Bishanpal	ਬਿਸ਼ਨਪਾਲ	Fostered by God
Birinder	ਬੀਰਿੰਦਰ	Lord of Braves
Birpal	ਬੀਰਪਾਲ	Fosterer of Braves
Birprem	ਬੀਰਪ੍ਰੇਮ	Love for Braves
Braham	ਬ੍ਰਹਮ	Supreme God
Brahampal	ਬ੍ਰਹਮਪਾਲ	God Fosterer
Braham Sarup	ਬ੍ਰਹਮਸਰੂਪ	God appearance
Brahamjeet	ਬ੍ਰਹਮਜੀਤ	Victory of God
Brahampreet	ਬ੍ਰਹਮਪ੍ਰੀਤ	Love for Supreme God
Brahamdev	ਬ੍ਰਹਮਦੇਵ	Supreme God
Budhjeet	ਬੁਧਜੀਤ	Victory for wisdom
Budhjiwan	ਬੁਧਜੀਵਨ	Wise life.
Budhjoti	ਬੁਧਜੋਤਿ	Light of Wisdom

ੴ

C ਚ

Chanpreet	ਚਨਪ੍ਰੀਤ	Love for Moon
Charandeep	ਚਰਨਦੀਪ	Light of (God's) feet
Charanjit	ਚਰਨਜੀਤ	Victory for (God's) feet
Charanpreet	ਚਰਨਪ੍ਰੀਤ	Love for God's feet
Chandan	ਚੰਦਨ	Sandal
Chandanwant	ਚੰਦਨਵੰਤ	Full of Sandal smell
Chandni	ਚਾਂਦਨੀ	moonlight
Chanchal	ਚੰਚਲ	Transient, agile, lively, playful
Charankanwal	ਚਰਨਕੰਵਲ	Lotus-like feet
Charanpal	ਚਰਨਪਾਲ	Fostered by (God's) feet
Chakradhar	ਚਕੱਰਧਰ	Lord Vishnu
Chakrapani	ਚਕੱਰਪਾਣਿ	Lord Vishnu
Chamanroop	ਚਮਨਰੂਪ	Beautiful like Garden
Chaman	ਚਮਨ	Garden
Chanderbhan	ਚੰਦਰਭਾਨ	Moon on forehead-Shiva
Chander Mohan	ਚੰਦਰ ਮੋਹਨ	Attracture like Moon

ੴ

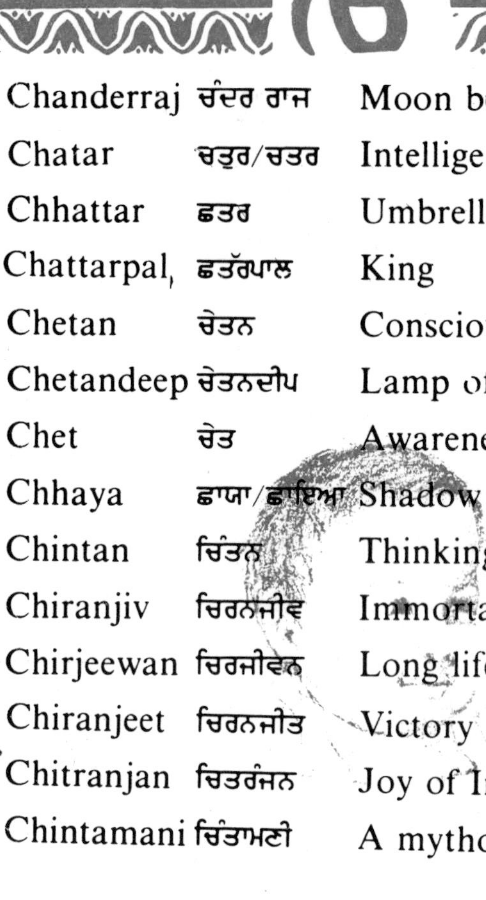

Chanderraj	ਚੰਦਰ ਰਾਜ	Moon beam
Chatar	ਚਤੁਰ/ਚਤਰ	Intelligent
Chhattar	ਛਤਰ	Umbrella, Sceptre
Chattarpal,	ਛਤੱਰਪਾਲ	King
Chetan	ਚੇਤਨ	Conscious
Chetandeep	ਚੇਤਨਦੀਪ	Lamp of consciousness
Chet	ਚੇਤ	Awareness
Chhaya	ਛਾਯਾ/ਛਾਇਆ	Shadow
Chintan	ਚਿੰਤਨ	Thinking, Meditation
Chiranjiv	ਚਿਰਨਜੀਵ	Immortal
Chirjeewan	ਚਿਰਜੀਵਨ	Long life, Everlasting life
Chiranjeet	ਚਿਰਨਜੀਤ	Victory for ever
Chitranjan	ਚਿਤਰੰਜਨ	Joy of Inner mind
Chintamani	ਚਿੰਤਾਮਣੀ	A mythological gem

ੴ

D ਦ

Dayal	ਦਿਆਲ/ਦਯਾਲ	Kind
Dayanidhan	ਦਿਆਨਿਧਾਨ	Abode of Kindness
Dayabir	ਦਇਆਬੀਰ	Brave in kindness
Dayasheel	ਦਇਆਸ਼ੀਲ	Kind-hearted
Daljeet	ਦਲਜੀਤ	Team-victory
Dalmeet	ਦਲਮੀਤ	Team-friend
Darpreet	ਦਰਪ੍ਰੀਤ	Love for (God's) door
Daya	ਦਯਾ ਦਇਆ	Kindness
Dayaprakash	ਦਇਆਪ੍ਰਕਾਸ਼	Light of kindness
Damanjit	ਦਮਨਜੀਤ	Victory over suppression
Dayawant	ਦਇਆਵੰਤ	Full of Kindness
Darbar	ਦਰਬਾਰ	Royal Court
Dalbir	ਦਲਬੀਰ	Hero of the team
Daljodh	ਦਲਜੋਧ	Team Fighter
Darshan	ਦਰਸ਼ਨ	Appearance visiting of a holy shrine.
Datar	ਦਾਤਾਰ	Benefactor God

ੴ

Devinder	ਦੇਵਿੰਦਰ	God
Devinderpal	ਦੇਵਿੰਦਰਪਾਲ	Fostered by God
Deepak	ਦੀਪਕ	Lamp
Deepkanwal	ਦੀਪਕੰਵਲ	Bright Lotus
Deepmohan	ਦੀਪਮੋਹਨ	Very attractive
Dev	ਦੇਵ	God, deity
Devi	ਦੇਵੀ	Goddess
Devraj	ਦੇਵਰਾਜ	Lord
Deepti	ਦੀਪਤੀ	Lustre
Divakar	ਦਿਵਾਕਰ	Sun
Deen Dayal	ਦੀਨਦਿਆਲ	Kind of the poor
Devjeet	ਦੇਵਜੀਤ	Victorious God
Devpreet	ਦੇਵਪ੍ਰੀਤ	Love for God
Devasheesh	ਦੇਵਅਸ਼ੀਸ਼	Blessings of God
Digvijay	ਦਿਗਵਿਜੈ	Conquest of all directions
Digpal	ਦਿਗਪਾਲ	Protector of all directions
Dhanwant	ਧਨਵੰਤ	Wealthy
Dharam	ਧਰਮ	Religion, faith, duty.
Dharambir	ਧਰਮਬੀਰ	Brave in doing his duty

ੴ

Dharampreet	ਧਰਮਪ੍ਰੀਤ	Love of faith
Dharamdev	ਧਰਮਦੇਵ	God of Faith
Dharamsheel	ਧਰਮਸ਼ੀਲ	Religious
Dharamdeep	ਧਰਮਦੀਪ	Lamp of Religion
Dharampal	ਧਰਮਪਾਲ	Fosterer of Religion
Dharaminder	ਧਰਮਿੰਦਰ	God of faith
Dhian	ਧਿਆਨ	Meditation
Dhianjot	ਧਿਆਨਜੋਤ	Light of meditation
Dhiraj	ਧੀਰਜ	Patience
Dhirajwant	ਧੀਰਜਵੰਤ	Full of Patience
Dhanpat	ਧਨਪਤ	Wealthy
Dharamsarup	ਧਰਮਸਰੂਪ	Religious appearance
Dipinder	ਦੀਪਿੰਦਰ	Radiant God
Dilpreet	ਦਿਲਪ੍ਰੀਤ	Hearty Love
Divya Jyoti	ਦਿਵਯਜੋਤਿ	Divine Light
Divjot	ਦਿਵਜੋਤ	Divine light
Disha	ਦਿਸ਼ਾ	Direction
Dilawar	ਦਿਲਾਵਰ	Bold, Brave

Dinesh	ਦਿਨੇਸ਼	Sun
Diler	ਦਿਲੇਰ	Courageous
Dilip	ਦਿਲੀਪ	King
Dilbagh	ਦਿਲਬਾਗ	Delighted
Didar	ਦੀਦਾਰ	Appearance, Sight, View
Deepshikha	ਦੀਪਸ਼ਿਖਾ	Flame of Lamp
Dhanbir	ਧਨਬੀਰ	Brave in Wealth

E ਏ

Ekamjeet	ਏਕਮਜੀਤ	Victory of one God
Ekampreet	ਏਕਮਪ੍ਰੀਤ	Love for one God
Ekambir	ਏਕਮਬੀਰ	One brave God
Ekant	ਏਕਾਂਤ	Solitude
Ekaagar	ਏਕਾਗਰ	Resolute
Ekjot	ਏਕਜੋਤ	God is one
Ekroop	ਏਕਰੂਪ	One appearance
Ekta	ਏਕਤਾ	Unity

ੴ

F ਫ

Falak ਫਲਕ Sky

Fateh ਫਤਰ Victory

Fatehbir ਫਤਹਬੀਰ Victorious Brave

Faqir ਫ਼ਕੀਰ Saint

G ਗ

Gagan ਗਗਨ Sky

Gaganpreet ਗਗਨਪ੍ਰੀਤ Love of sky

Gaganbir ਗਗਨਬੀਰ Sky Brave

Gagandeep ਗਗਨਦੀਤ Sky Lamp

Gaganjit ਗਗਨਜੀਤ Sky Victor

Garima ਗਰਿਮਾ Dignity

Gaurav ਗੌਰਵ Pride, Glory

Gauravdeep ਗੌਰਵਦੀਪ Lamp of Glory

Gajinder ਗਜਿੰਦਰ God of Elephants, Indra

Gautam ਗੌਤਮ Name of a Rishi, Lord Budha

ੴ

Geetika	ਗੀਤਿਕਾ	Lyrical
Gian	ਗਿਆਨ	Knowledge
Giandeep	ਗਿਆਨਦੀਪ	Lamp of knowledge.
Gianpreet	ਗਿਆਨਪ੍ਰੀਤ	Love of knowledge
Gianjot	ਗਿਆਨਜੋਤ	Light of knowledge
Girdhar	ਗਿਰਧਰ	Lord Krishna
Girish	ਗਿਰੀਸ਼	Lord of mountains, Shiva
Gitanjali	ਗੀਤਾਂਜਲੀ	An offering of songs
Gobind	ਗੋਬਿੰਦ	God
Gopal	ਗੋਪਾਲ	Krishna, God
Gurmeet	ਗੁਰਮੀਤ	Friend of the Guru
Gunjan	ਗੁੰਜਨ	Humming sound
Gurdev	ਗੁਰਦੇਵ	Lord Guru
Gurjas	ਗੁਰਜਸ	Glory of the Guru
Gurjeet	ਗੁਰਜੀਤ	Victory of the Guru
Gurjinder	ਗੁਰਜਿੰਦਰ	Victory of the Guru
Gurleen	ਗੁਰਲੀਨ	Absorbed in the Guru
Gurpal	ਗੁਰਪਾਲ	Fostered by the Guru

ੴ

Gurpreet	ਗੁਰਪ੍ਰੀਤ	Love of the Guru
Gurdarshan	ਗੁਰਦਰਸ਼ਨ	Appearance of the Guru
Gursimran	ਗੁਰਸਿਮਰਨ	Remembrance of the Guru
Gursheel	ਗੁਰਸ਼ੀਲ	Modesty given by the Guru
Gurneet	ਗੁਰਨੀਤ	Moral given by the Guru
Gurtej	ਗੁਰਤੇਜ	Glory of the Guru
Gurdeep	ਗੁਰਦੀਪ	Lamp of the Guru
Gulzar	ਗੁਲਜ਼ਾਰ	Garden
Gurnam	ਗੁਰਨਾਮ	Name of the Guru
Gurmukh	ਗੁਰਮੁਖ	Pious man
Gungeet	ਗੁਣਗੀਤ	Song of virtues
Gunpreet	ਗੁਣਪ੍ਰੀਤ	Love of virtues
Gunwant	ਗੁਣਵੰਤ	Virtues
Guneet	ਗੁਣੀਤ	Full of virtues
Guriqbal	ਗੁਰਇਕਬਾਲ	Glory of the Guru
Gurupdesh	ਗੁਰਉਪਦੇਸ਼	Teaching of the Guru
Gurinder	ਗੁਰਿੰਦਰ	Lord Guru
Gurwinder	ਗੁਰਵਿੰਦਰ	Lord Guru
Gursharan	ਗੁਰਸ਼ਰਨ	In the Shelter of the Guru

ੴ

Gurcharan	ਗੁਰਚਰਨ	Guru's feet
Gursimran	ਗੁਰਸਿਮਰਨ	Remembrance of the Guru
Gursevak	ਗੁਰਸੇਵਕ	In the service of the Guru
Gurukirat	ਗੁਰਕੀਰਤ	Praise of the Guru
Gurjit	ਗੁਰਜੀਤ	Victory of the Guru
Gurdayal	ਗੁਰਦਿਆਲ	Kind Guru
Gurbaksh	ਗੁਰਬਖਸ਼	Gift of the Guru
Gurbir	ਗੁਰਬੀਰ	Bravery of the Guru
Gurbhagat	ਗੁਰਭਗਤ	Devotion for the Guru
Gurbachan	ਗੁਰਬਚਨ	words of The Guru
Gulwant	ਗੁਲਵੰਤ	Beautiful like flowers
Gulab	ਗੁਲਾਬ	Rose
Guninder	ਗੁਨਿੰਦਰ	Lord of virtues
Gunratan	ਗੁਣਰਤਨ	Jewel of virtues
Gyandev	ਗਿਆਨਦੇਵ	Lord of knowledge
Gyanprakash	ਗਿਆਨਪ੍ਰਕਾਸ਼	Light of knowledge
Gyanender	ਗਿਆਨਿੰਦਰ	Lord of knowledge.
Gyanpreet	ਗਿਆਨਪ੍ਰੀਤ	Love of knowledge

ੴ

H ਹ

Harjee	ਹਰਜੀ	God
Harjeet	ਹਰਜੀਤ	Victory of God
Harjinder	ਹਰਜਿੰਦਰ	Life gifted by God
Harjot	ਹਰਜੋਤ	Light of God
Harbinder	ਹਰਬਿੰਦਰ	Engrossed in God
Harkirat	ਹਰਕੀਰਤ	Praise of God
Harmanjit	ਹਰਮਨਜੀਤ	Victory of God's Heart
Harmeet	ਹਰਮੀਤ	Friend of God
Harmohan	ਹਰਮੋਹਨ	Charming God
Harpreet	ਹਰਪ੍ਰੀਤ	Love of God
Harpuneet	ਹਰਪੁਨੀਤ	Pure like God
Harsimran	ਹਰਸਿਮਰਨ	Remembrance of God
Harsimrit	ਹਰਸਿਮ੍ਰਿਤ	Memory of God
Harshit	ਹਰਸ਼ਿਤ	Joyous
Harshbir	ਹਰਸ਼ਬੀਰ	Happy brave
Harshwardhan	ਹਰਸ਼ਵਰਧਨ	Fosterer of Joy
Harish	ਹਰੀਸ਼	God

ੴ

Hariprakash	ਹਰੀਪ੍ਰਕਾਸ਼	God's light
Harit	ਹਰਿਤ	Green
Harsh	ਹਰਸ਼	Happiness
Hari Amrit	ਹਰਿਅੰਮ੍ਰਿਤ	Nectar of God
Harisharan	ਹਰਿਸ਼ਰਨ	In the Shelter of God
Harikishan	ਹਰਿਕਿਸ਼ਨ	Lord Krishna
Harisaroop	ਹਰਿਸਰੂਪ	Appearance of God
Harnam	ਹਰਨਾਮ	Name of God
Harikiran	ਹਰਿਕਿਰਨ	Ray of God
Harchand	ਹਰਚੰਦ	Moon-like God
Harjiwan	ਹਰਜੀਵਨ	Life with God
Harjodh	ਹਰਜੋਤ	Brave like God
Hartirath	ਹਰਤੀਰਥ	Holy place of God
Harbhajan	ਹਰਭਜਨ	Hymns of God
Hartej	ਹਰਤੇਜ	Glow of God
Hardarshan	ਹਰਦਰਸ਼ਨ	Appearance of God
Hardayal	ਹਰਦਿਆਲ	Kind God
Hardeep	ਹਰਦੀਪ	Light of God

ੴ

Hardev	ਹਰਦੇਵ	Supreme God
Harpal	ਹਰਪਾਲ	God Fosterer
Harbir	ਹਰਬੀਰ	Brave like God
Harmandir	ਹਰਮੇਂਦਿਰ	Temple of God
Harleen	ਹਰਲੀਨ	Engrossed in God
Harbans	ਹਰਬੰਸ	Family of God
Hirdeypal	ਹਿਰਦੇਪਾਲ	Heart Fosterer
Harlochan	ਹਰਲੋਚਨ	Eyes of God
Hem	ਹੇਮ	Gold
Hemant	ਹੇਮੰਤ	Winter season
Heminder	ਹੇਮਿੰਦਰ	Lord of gold
Hitesh	ਹਿਤੇਸ਼	Benevolent God
Harinder	ਹਰਿੰਦਰ	God
Hitinder	ਹਿਤਿੰਦਰ	Benevolant God
Hirender	ਹਿਰੇਂਦਰ	Lord of Diamonds
Hira	ਹੀਰਾ	Diamond
Himmat	ਹਿੰਮਤ	Courage

ੴ

I ਇ

Ila	ਇਲਾ	The earth, speech, the Goddess' Parvati
Inderbir	ਇੰਦਰਬੀਰ	Lord of Bravery
Inderdeep	ਇੰਦਰਦੀਪ	Light of the Lord
Inderjit	ਇੰਦਰਜੀਤ	Victory of the Lord
Indermohan	ਇੰਦਰਮੋਹਨ	Charm of the Lord.
Inderpal	ਇੰਦਰਪਾਲ	Fostered by the Lord
Inderpreet	ਇੰਦਰਪ੍ਰੀਤ	Love for the Lord
Indivar	ਇੰਦੀਵਰ	Blue lotus
Indu	ਇੰਦੂ	Moon
Induprakash	ਇੰਦੂਪ੍ਰਕਾਸ਼	Moonlight
Ira	ਇਰਾ	The earth
Ishpreet	ਈਸ਼ਪ੍ਰੀਤ	Love of God
Isha	ਈਸ਼ਾ	Goddess
Ishtpreet	ਇਸਟਪ੍ਰੀਤ	Love of God
Ishwar	ਇਸ਼ਵਰ	God
Ishar	ਈਸ਼ਰ	God
Iqbal	ਇਕਬਾਲ	Glory

ੴ

J ਜ

Jasjeet	ਜਸਜੀਤ	Victory of Glory
Jasleen	ਜਸਲੀਨ	Absorbed in the glory of God
Jasmeet	ਜਸਮੀਤ	Friend of the glory
Jasmine	ਜਸਮੀਨ	A flower
Jaspal	ਜਸਪਾਲ	Fosterer of glory
Jasraj	ਜਸਰਾਜ	King of glory
Jaspreet	ਜਸਪ੍ਰੀਤ	Love of glory
Jaswinder	ਜਸਵਿੰਦਰ	Lord of glory
Jatinder	ਜਤਿੰਦਰ	Lord of purity
Jatin	ਜਤਿਨ	An ascetic
Jatinderpal	ਜਤਿੰਦਰਪਾਲ	Protected by God
Jyoti	ਜਯੋਤਿ/ਜੋਤੀ	Flame
Jagjit	ਜਗਜੀਤ	Victor of the world
Jagmeet	ਜਗਮੀਤ	Friend of the world
Jagpreet	ਜਗਪ੍ਰੀਤ	Love of the world
Jagtar	ਜਗਤਾਰ	Emancipator of the world

ੴ

Jaideep	ਜੈਦੀਪ	Lamp of victory
Jaidev	ਜੈਦੇਵ	Lord of victory
Jaikiran	ਜੈਕਿਰਨ	Ray of victory
Jasbir	ਜਸਬੀਰ	Glorious brave
Jasdeep	ਜਸਦੀਪ	Lamp of glory
Japjeet	ਜਪਜੀਤ	Victory of adoration
Jagat	ਜਗਤ	World
Jagatprakash	ਜਗਤਪ੍ਰਕਾਸ਼	Light of the world
Jastej	ਜਸਤੇਜ	Glow of glory
Jasminder	ਜਸਮਿੰਦਰ	God of glory
Jasroop	ਜਸਰੂਪ	Face of glory
Jastaran	ਜਸਤਰਨ	Floating in glory
Jaskirat	ਜਸਕੀਰਤ	Praise of glory
Jagriti	ਜਾਗ੍ਰਿਤੀ	Awakening
Jaipal	ਜੈਪਾਲ	Protector of victory
Jairaj	ਜੈਰਾਜ	Lord of victory
Jaisudha	ਜੈਸੁਧਾ	Nectar of victory
Jaisukhbir	ਜੈਸੁਖਬੀਰ	Victorious happy, brave

ੴ

Jaiwant	ਜੈਵੰਤ	Vicotorious
Janeesh	ਜਨੀਸ਼	Lord of the people
Japneet	ਜਪਨੀਤ	Absorbed in adoration
Jaskirpal	ਜਸਕਿਰਪਾਲ	Glory of Kind God
Jaswant	ਜਸਵੰਤ	Full of glory
Jagjeevan	ਜਗਜੀਵਨ	Life in the world
Jagatjeet	ਜਗਤਜੀਤ	Victorious of the world
Jagatpal	ਜਗਤਪਾਲ	Fosterer of the world
Jagatpreet	ਜਗਤਪ੍ਰੀਤ	Love of the world
Jagtaran	ਜਗਤਾਰਨ	Emancip ator of the world
Jagdish	ਜਗਦੀਸ਼	Lord of the world
Jagdeep	ਜਗਦੀਪ	Light of the world
Jagmohan	ਜਗਮੋਹਨ	Charm of the world
Jagdev	ਜਗਦੇਵ	God of the world
Janak	ਜਨਕ	Father
Janpal	ਜਨਪਾਲ	Fosterer of the people
Janraj	ਜਨਰਾਜ	King of the people
Janinder	ਜਨਿੰਦਰ	Lord
Japinder	ਜਪਿੰਦਰ	Praise of God

ੴ

Japleen	ਜਪਲੀਨ	Engrossed in Praise
Jaipreet	ਜੈਪ੍ਰੀਤ	Love of victory
Joginder	ਜੋਗਿੰਦਰ	Master of Yoga
Juhi	ਜੂਹੀ	A Flower
Jairatan	ਜੈਰਤਨ	Jewel of Victory
Jyotsna	ਜਿਓਤਸਨਾ	Moonlight
Jeet	ਜੀਤ	Victory
Jiwan	ਜੀਵਨ	Life
Jiwanpal	ਜੀਵਨਪਾਲ	Fosterer of life
Jiwanpreet	ਜੀਵਨਪ੍ਰੀਤ	Love of life.
Jotipal	ਜੋਤੀਪਾਲ	Fosterer of light
Jorawar	ਜੋਰਾਵਰ	Powerful
Jagpreet	ਜਗਪ੍ਰੀਤ	Love for the world
Jugraj	ਜੁਗਰਾਜ	King of the age
Jujhar	ਜੁਝਾਰ	Warrior

ੴ

K ਕ

Kamal	ਕਮਲ	Lotus
Kanwal	ਕੰਵਲ	Lotus
Kanwaldeep	ਕੰਵਲਦੀਪ	Light of lotus
Kanwalpreet	ਕੰਵਲਪ੍ਰੀਤ	Love of Lotus
Kamlesh	ਕਮਲੇਸ਼	God of Lotus
Kamalpreet	ਕਮਲਪ੍ਰੀਤ	Love of Lotus
Kanwarbir	ਕੰਵਰਬੀਰ	Brave Prince
Kanwarjeet	ਕੰਵਰਜੀਤ	Victory of Prince
Karamjeet	ਕਰਮਜੀਤ	Victory of deeds
Karam	ਕਰਮ	Deed, Action, Destiny
Karan	ਕਰਨ	Ear, A character in Mahabharata
Kanwardeep	ਕੰਵਰਦੀਪ	Light of prince
Kanwarpreet	ਕੰਵਰਪ੍ਰੀਤ	Love of prince
Kanika	ਕਨਿਕਾ	An atom, a particle
Kalika	ਕਲਿਕਾ	A bud
Karambir	ਕਰਮਬੀਰ	Brave of deeds

ੴ

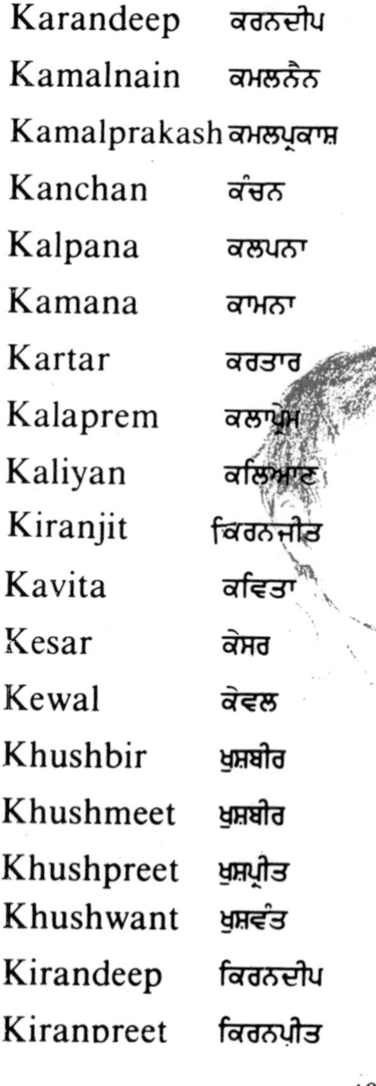

Karandeep	ਕਰਨਦੀਪ	Light of helm
Kamalnain	ਕਮਲਨੈਨ	Lotus-eyed
Kamalprakash	ਕਮਲਪ੍ਰਕਾਸ਼	Lotus-light
Kanchan	ਕੰਚਨ	Gold
Kalpana	ਕਲਪਨਾ	Imagination
Kamana	ਕਾਮਨਾ	Desire
Kartar	ਕਰਤਾਰ	Creator
Kalaprem	ਕਲਾਪ੍ਰੇਮ	Love of Art
Kaliyan	ਕਲਿਆਣ	welfare
Kiranjit	ਕਿਰਨਜੀਤ	Victory over rays
Kavita	ਕਵਿਤਾ	Poetry
Kesar	ਕੇਸਰ	Saffron
Kewal	ਕੇਵਲ	Only
Khushbir	ਖੁਸ਼ਬੀਰ	Happy Brave
Khushmeet	ਖੁਸ਼ਬੀਰ	Happy friend
Khushpreet	ਖੁਸ਼ਪ੍ਰੀਤ	Love for happiness
Khushwant	ਖੁਸ਼ਵੰਤ	Full of happiness
Kirandeep	ਕਿਰਨਦੀਪ	Ray of light
Kiranpreet	ਕਿਰਨਪ੍ਰੀਤ	Love of Light

ੴ

Kishan	ਕਿਸ਼ਨ	Lord Krishna
Kishan Prakash	ਕਿਸ਼ਨ ਪ੍ਰਕਾਸ਼	God's light
Kirpal	ਕ੍ਰਿਪਾਲ	Kind
Kirat	ਕੀਰਤ	Praise
Kirtan	ਕੀਰਤਨ	Devotional Singing
Komal	ਕੋਮਲ	Soft, tender
Komaljeet	ਕੋਮਲਜੀਤ	Victory for softness
Komalpreet	ਕੋਮਲਪ੍ਰੀਤ	Love for softness
Kultar	ਕੁਲਤਾਰ	Emancipator of Family
Kultaran	ਕੁਲਤਾਰਨ	Emancipation of family
Kuldeep	ਕੁਲਦੀਪ	Light of family
Kulmohan	ਕੁਲਮੋਹਨ	Family charm
Kuljeet	ਕੁਲਜੀਤ	Victory of family
Kulpreet	ਕੁਲਪ੍ਰੀਤ	Love of family
Kusum	ਕੁਸੁਮ	Kusum

ੴ

L ਲ

Lakhbir	ਲਖਬੀਰ	Brave in lakhs
Lalkar	ਲਲਕਾਰ	Challenge
Lalit	ਲਲਿਤ	Fine
Lakhminder	ਲਖਮਿੰਦਰ	Lord of lakhs
Lachhman	ਲਛਮਣ	Younger brother of Ram
Lajpal	ਲਾਜਪਾਲ	Protector of honour
Lajpreet	ਲਾਜਪ੍ਰੀਤ	Love of honour
Labh	ਲਾਭ	Profit
Livchetan	ਲਿਵਚੇਤਨ	Conscious in adoration
Livtar	ਲਿਵਤਾਰ	Adoration
Livpreet	ਲਿਵਪ੍ਰੀਤ	Love of adoration
Livjot	ਲਿਵਜੋਤ	Light of adoration
Lovleen	ਲਵਲੀਨ	Absorbed in adoration
Lokmeet	ਲੋਕਮੀਤ	Friend of the people
Lochan	ਲੋਚਨ	Eyes
Lokpal	ਲੋਕਪਾਲ	Protector of the people
Lokesh	ਲੋਕੇਸ਼	God of the people

ੴ

Lokraj	ਲੋਕਰਾਜ	Democracy
Loklaj	ਲੋਕਲਾਜ	Honour of the people
Lajwant	ਲਾਜਵੰਤ	Honourable
Laima	ਲਾਲਿਮਾ	Redness
Lekhraj	ਲੇਖਰਾਜ	God of death

M ਮ

Maheep	ਮਹੀਪ	King
Mandeep	ਮਨਦੀਪ	Light of mind
Madhupreet	ਮਧੁਪ੍ਰੀਤ	Love of honey/Sweetness
Mahinder	ਮਹਿੰਦਰ	Lord of earth
Mahipal	ਮਹਿਪਾਲ	Protector of earth
Mala	ਮਾਲਾ	Garland, a wreath
Manak	ਮਾਣਕ	Ruby
Manavdeep	ਮਾਨਵਦੀਪ	Light of humanity
Maninder	ਮਨਿੰਦਰ	Lord of mind
Manjot	ਮਨਜੋਤ	Flame of mind
Manjit	ਮਨਜੀਤ	Victory of mind

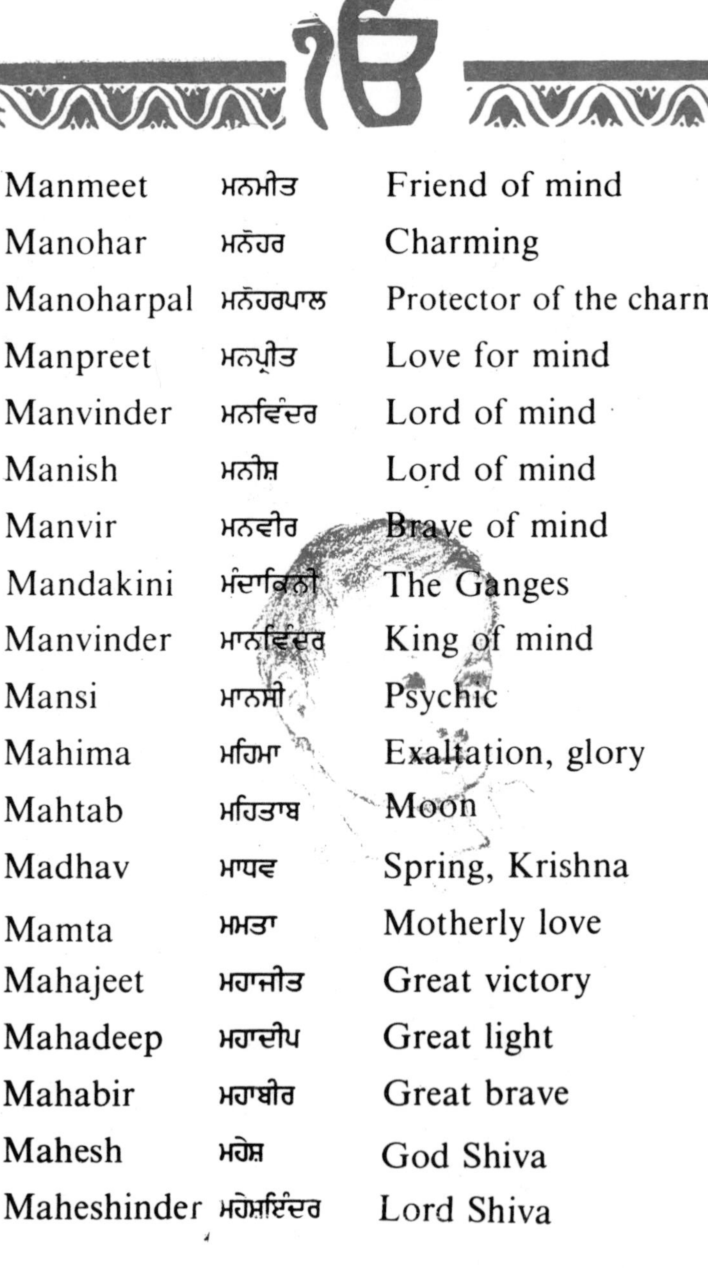

Manmeet	ਮਨਮੀਤ	Friend of mind
Manohar	ਮਨੋਹਰ	Charming
Manoharpal	ਮਨੋਹਰਪਾਲ	Protector of the charming
Manpreet	ਮਨਪ੍ਰੀਤ	Love for mind
Manvinder	ਮਨਵਿੰਦਰ	Lord of mind
Manish	ਮਨੀਸ਼	Lord of mind
Manvir	ਮਨਵੀਰ	Brave of mind
Mandakini	ਮੰਦਾਕਿਨੀ	The Ganges
Manvinder	ਮਾਨਵਿੰਦਰ	King of mind
Mansi	ਮਾਨਸੀ	Psychic
Mahima	ਮਹਿਮਾ	Exaltation, glory
Mahtab	ਮਹਿਤਾਬ	Moon
Madhav	ਮਾਧਵ	Spring, Krishna
Mamta	ਮਮਤਾ	Motherly love
Mahajeet	ਮਹਾਜੀਤ	Great victory
Mahadeep	ਮਹਾਦੀਪ	Great light
Mahabir	ਮਹਾਬੀਰ	Great brave
Mahesh	ਮਹੇਸ਼	God Shiva
Maheshinder	ਮਹੇਸ਼ਇੰਦਰ	Lord Shiva

ੴ

Matinder	ਮਤਿੰਦਰ	Lord of wisdom
Madan	ਮਦਨ	Cupid, Kamdev
Madanjeet	ਮਦਨਜੀਤ	Victory on cupid
Mansheetal	ਮਨਸੀਤਲ	Satisfaction of mind
Manjinder	ਮਨਜਿੰਦਰ	Lord of mind
Mantej	ਮਨਤੇਜ	Glow of mind
Mandev	ਮਨਦੇਵ	God of mind
Manmohan	ਮਨਮੋਹਨ	Charming
Manasjeet	ਮਾਨਸਜੀਤ	Victory of mind
Manasjot	ਮਾਨਸਜੋਤ	Flame of mind
Manasdeep	ਮਾਨਸਦੀਪ	Ligt of mind
Manaspreet	ਮਾਨਸਪ੍ਰੀਤ	Love of mind
Manavinder	ਮਾਨਵਿੰਦਰ	Lord of humanity
Manavpreet	ਮਾਨਵਪ੍ਰੀਤ	Love of humanity
Manavmeet	ਮਾਨਵਮੀਤ	Friend of humanity
Mangal	ਮੰਗਲ	Welfare
Mangaljot	ਮੰਗਲਜੋਤ	Flame of well-being
Manoj	ਮਨੋਜ	Cupid, Kamdev
Meenakshi	ਮੀਨਾਕਸ਼ੀ	Fish-eyed

ੴ

Meeta	ਮੀਤਾ	Friend
Meetkamal	ਮੀਤਕਮਲ	Friend of lotus
Meghdeep	ਮੇਘਦੀਪ	Lightning
Mehar	ਮੇਹਰ	Kindness
Meharpal	ਮੇਹਰਪਾਲ	Protected by kindness
Mina	ਮੀਨਾ	Enamel-work
Mohit	ਮੋਹਿਤ	Fascinated
Mukt/Mukat	ਮੁਕਤ	Emancipated
Mohini	ਮੋਹਿਨੀ	Attractive, Charming
Mohan	ਮੋਹਨ	Charming
Mohanjeet	ਮੋਹਨਜੀਤ	Victory of Charm
Mohanpal	ਮੋਹਨਪਾਲ	Protector of the Charming
Mohanpreet	ਮੋਹਨਪ੍ਰੀਤ	Love of Charm
Mohanbir	ਮੋਹਨਬੀਰ	Charming Brave
Mrigind	ਮ੍ਰਿਗਿੰਦ	Lion
Mukul	ਮੁਕੁਲ	Bud, Blosson
Muknd	ਮੁਕੰਦ	Jewel, Krishna
Mukundjeet	ਮੁਕੰਦਜੀਤ	Jewel victor
Mukesh	ਮੁਕੇਸ਼	Cupid

ੴ

N ਨ

Naindeep	ਨੈਨਦੀਪ	Eyes full of light
Namarta	ਨਮ੍ਰਿਤਾ	Modesty
Nanak	ਨਾਨਕ	Name of the first Sikh Guru
Navjot	ਨਵਜੋਤ	New flame
Navleen	ਨਵਲੀਨ	New engrossed
Navneet	ਨਵਨੀਤ	Butter
Navpreet	ਨਵਪ੍ਰੀਤ	New love
Navdeep	ਨਵਦੀਪ	New light
Naininder	ਨੈਨਿੰਦਰ	God in eyes
Nalin	ਨਲਿਨ	Lotus
Nandan	ਨੰਦਨ	Son,
Nandini	ਨੰਦਿਨੀ	Daughter
Nandit	ਨੰਦਿਤ	Delighted
Narinder	ਨਰਿੰਦਰ	King
Narinderjeet	ਨਰਿੰਦਰਜੀਤ	Victory over king

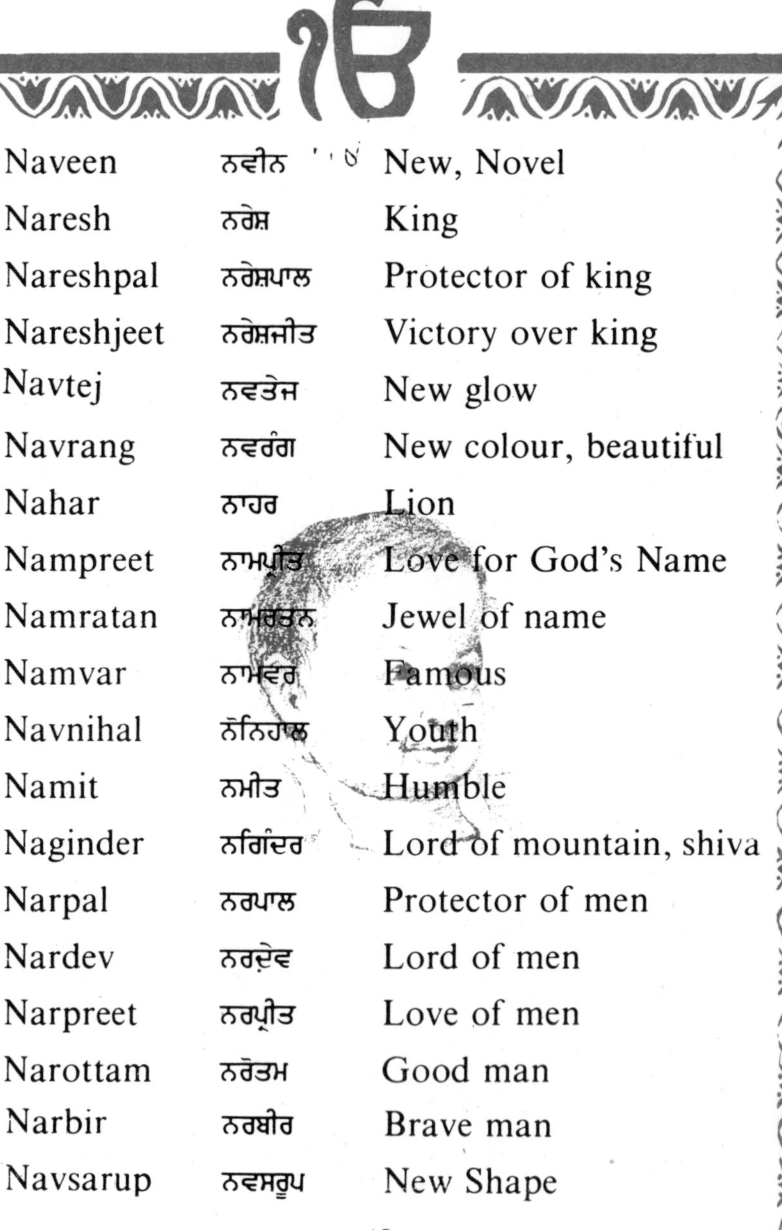

Naveen	ਨਵੀਨ	New, Novel
Naresh	ਨਰੇਸ਼	King
Nareshpal	ਨਰੇਸ਼ਪਾਲ	Protector of king
Nareshjeet	ਨਰੇਸ਼ਜੀਤ	Victory over king
Navtej	ਨਵਤੇਜ	New glow
Navrang	ਨਵਰੰਗ	New colour, beautiful
Nahar	ਨਾਹਰ	Lion
Nampreet	ਨਾਮਪ੍ਰੀਤ	Love for God's Name
Namratan	ਨਾਮਰਤਨ	Jewel of name
Namvar	ਨਾਮਵਰ	Famous
Navnihal	ਨੌਨਿਹਾਲ	Youth
Namit	ਨਮੀਤ	Humble
Naginder	ਨਗਿੰਦਰ	Lord of mountain, shiva
Narpal	ਨਰਪਾਲ	Protector of men
Nardev	ਨਰਦੇਵ	Lord of men
Narpreet	ਨਰਪ੍ਰੀਤ	Love of men
Narottam	ਨਰੋਤਮ	Good man
Narbir	ਨਰਬੀਰ	Brave man
Navsarup	ਨਵਸਰੂਪ	New Shape

ੴ

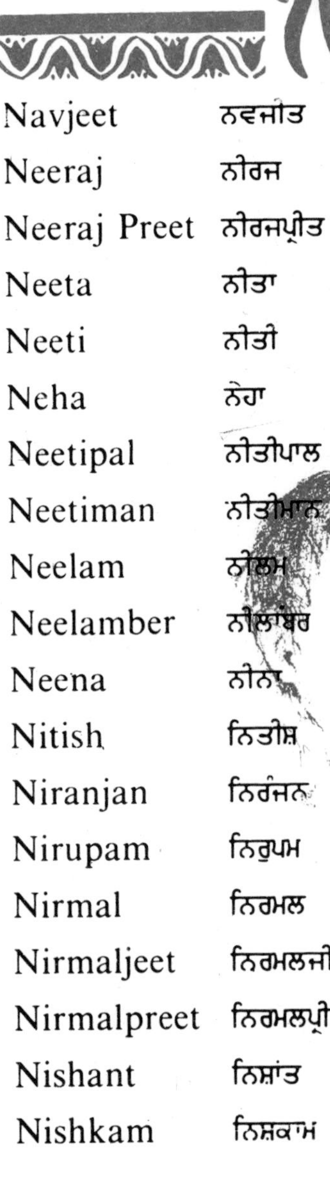

Navjeet	ਨਵਜੀਤ	New victory
Neeraj	ਨੀਰਜ	Lotus
Neeraj Preet	ਨੀਰਜਪ੍ਰੀਤ	Love of lotus
Neeta	ਨੀਤਾ	Upright
Neeti	ਨੀਤੀ	Good behaviour
Neha	ਨੇਹਾ	Love
Neetipal	ਨੀਤੀਪਾਲ	Protecter of law
Neetiman	ਨੀਤੀਮਾਨ	Lawful
Neelam	ਨੀਲਮ	Sapphire
Neelamber	ਨੀਲਾਂਬਰ	Blue sky
Neena	ਨੀਨਾ	Lovely eyes
Nitish	ਨਿਤੀਸ਼	Master of right path
Niranjan	ਨਿਰੰਜਨ	Unblemished God
Nirupam	ਨਿਰੁਪਮ	Without camparison
Nirmal	ਨਿਰਮਲ	Pure
Nirmaljeet	ਨਿਰਮਲਜੀਤ	Victory of purity
Nirmalpreet	ਨਿਰਮਲਪ੍ਰੀਤ	Love of purity
Nishant	ਨਿਸ਼ਾਂਤ	Dawn
Nishkam	ਨਿਸ਼ਕਾਮ	Without desire

ੴ

Nihchal	ਨਿਹਚਲਹੈ	Firm
Nihal	ਨਿਹਾਲ	Delighted
Nirvair	ਨਿਰਵੈਰ	Without enmity
Nirbhay	ਨਿਰਭੈ	Without fear
Nirman	ਨਿਮਾਣ	Creation
Nirmolak	ਨਿਰਮੋਲਕ	Valueless
Nirlep	ਨਿਰਲੇਪ	Without attachment
Niket	ਨਿਕੇਤ	Home
Nirad	ਨੀਰਦ	Cloud
Nisha	ਨਿਸ਼ਾ	Night
Nripinder	ਨ੍ਰਿਪਇੰਦਰ	Lord of kings
Nripal	ਨ੍ਰਿਪਾਲ	King
Navkiran	ਨਵਕਿਰਨ	New rays

ੴ

O ੳ

Onkar	ਉਂਕਾਰ	God's name
Onkarpreet	ਉਂਕਾਰਪ੍ਰੀਤ	Love for God's name
Onkarjeet	ਉਂਕਾਰਜੀਤ	Victory for God's name
Opinder	ਉਪਿੰਦਰ	Proximity of God
Opkar	ਉਪਕਾਰ	Benificence

P ਪ

Patwant	ਪਤਵੰਤ	Full of honour
Pawan	ਪਵਨ	Air
Pawandeep	ਪਵਨਦੀਪ	Lamp in air
Parineet	ਪਰਿਣੀਤ	Wedded, married
Paridarshan	ਪਰਿਦਰਸ਼ਨ	Panoramic view
Paramjit	ਪਰਮਜੀਤ	Victory of supreme
Paramjot	ਪਰਮਜੋਤ	Flame of supreme
Parampreet	ਪਰਮਪ੍ਰੀਤ	Love of supreme

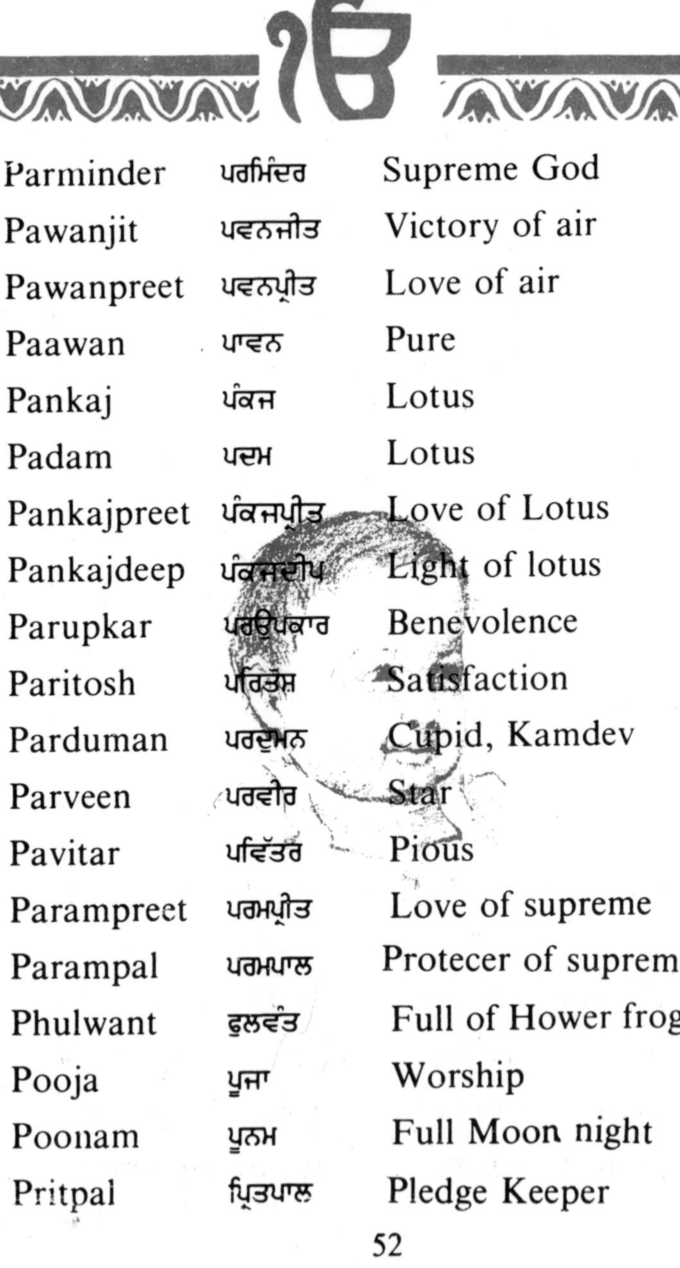

Parminder	ਪਰਮਿੰਦਰ	Supreme God
Pawanjit	ਪਵਨਜੀਤ	Victory of air
Pawanpreet	ਪਵਨਪ੍ਰੀਤ	Love of air
Paawan	ਪਾਵਨ	Pure
Pankaj	ਪੰਕਜ	Lotus
Padam	ਪਦਮ	Lotus
Pankajpreet	ਪੰਕਜਪ੍ਰੀਤ	Love of Lotus
Pankajdeep	ਪੰਕਜਦੀਪ	Light of lotus
Parupkar	ਪਰਉਪਕਾਰ	Benevolence
Paritosh	ਪਰਿਤੋਸ਼	Satisfaction
Parduman	ਪਰਦੂਮਨ	Cupid, Kamdev
Parveen	ਪਰਵੀਰ	Star
Pavitar	ਪਵਿੱਤਰ	Pious
Parampreet	ਪਰਮਪ੍ਰੀਤ	Love of supreme
Parampal	ਪਰਮਪਾਲ	Protecer of supreme
Phulwant	ਫੁਲਵੰਤ	Full of Hower frogrance
Pooja	ਪੂਜਾ	Worship
Poonam	ਪੂਨਮ	Full Moon night
Pritpal	ਪ੍ਰਿਤਪਾਲ	Pledge Keeper

ੴ

Praneet	ਪ੍ਰਣੀਤ	Written, composed
Prabh-simran	ਪ੍ਰਭਸਿਮਰਨ	Adoration of God
Prabhjot	ਪ੍ਰਭਜੋਤ	Flame of God
Prabhjit	ਪ੍ਰਭਜੀਤ	Victory of God
Prabodh	ਪ੍ਰਬੋਧ	Enlightenment
Pramod	ਪ੍ਰਮੋਦ	Delight, joy
Pratibha	ਪ੍ਰਤਿਭਾ	Talent, Genius
Preet	ਪ੍ਰੀਤ	Love
Pradeep	ਪ੍ਰਦੀਪ	A lamp
Prateek	ਪ੍ਰਤੀਕ	Symbol
Prabha	ਪ੍ਰਭਾ	Lustre
Prabhat	ਪ੍ਰਭਾਤ	Morning
Prabhatkiran	ਪ੍ਰਭਾਤਕਿਰਨ	Morning ray
Prafull	ਪ੍ਰਫੁੱਲ	Blooming
Pragya	ਪ੍ਰਗਿਆ	Wisdom
Prahlad	ਪ੍ਰਹਲਾਦ	Joy
Prajeet	ਪ੍ਰਜੀਤ	Kind
Prakash	ਪ੍ਰਕਾਸ਼	Light

ੴ

Pran	ਪ੍ਰਾਣ	Life
Prashant	ਪ੍ਰਸ਼ਾਂਤ	Calm
Prem	ਪ੍ਰੇਮ	Love
Premjeet	ਪ੍ਰੇਮਜੀਤ	Victory of love
Prempal	ਪ੍ਰੇਮਪਾਲ	Fosterer of love
Prakashdeep	ਪ੍ਰਕਾਸ਼ਦੀਪ	Lamp of light, light house
Prakashbir	ਪ੍ਰਕਾਸ਼ਬੀਰ	Famous, brave
Pratit	ਪ੍ਰਤੀਤ	Faith
Pradhan	ਪ੍ਰਧਾਨ	Head
Prabhmeet	ਪ੍ਰਭਮੀਤ	Friend of God
Prabhrup	ਪ੍ਰਭਰੂਪ	Appearance of God
Prabhakar	ਪ੍ਰਭਾਕਰ	Sun
Preetam	ਪ੍ਰੀਤਮ	Beloved
Preetamjeet	ਪ੍ਰੀਤਮਜੀਤ	Victory of beloved
Premdeep	ਪ੍ਰੇਮਦੀਪ	Lamp of love
Premprakash	ਪ੍ਰੇਮਪ੍ਰਕਾਸ਼	Light of love
Premwant	ਪ੍ਰੇਮਵੰਤ	Full of love
Prembir	ਪ੍ਰੇਮਬੀਰ	Brave in love
Prageet	ਪ੍ਰਗੀਤ	Song, lyric

ੴ

Puneet	ਪੁਨੀਤ	Pious
Puneetpal	ਪੁਨੀਤਪਾਲ	Fosterer of purity
Pushpinder	ਪੁਸ਼ਪਿੰਦਰ	God of flowers
Pushp preet	ਪੁਸ਼ਪ-ਪ੍ਰੀਤ	Love of flowers
Purshottam	ਪੁਰਸ਼ੋਤਮ	Best person
Puran	ਪੂਰਨ	Complete
Puran-gian	ਪੂਰਨਗਿਆਨ	Complete knowledge
Puranjeet	ਪੂਰਨਜੀਤ	Victory of complete
Puranjot	ਪੂਰਨਜੋਤ	Complete flame
Puranpreet	ਪੂਰਨਪ੍ਰੀਤ	Complete love
Pushpreet	ਪੁਸ਼ਪ੍ਰੀਤ	Love for flower

R ਰ

Rachneet	ਰਚਨੀਤ	Absorbed in creation
Rahul	ਰਾਹੁਲ	Name of the son of lord Budha
Rahuljit	ਰਾਹੁਲਜੀਤ	Victory for Rahul
Rahuldeep	ਰਾਹੁਲਦੀਪ	Light of Rahul
Rahulpreet	ਰਾਹੁਲਪ੍ਰੀਤ	Love of Rahul

ੴ

Rajdeep	ਰਾਜਦੀਪ	Lamp of Kingdom
Rajat	ਰਜਤ	Silver
Rajan	ਰਾਜਨ	King
Rashmi	ਰਸ਼ਮੀ	Ray
Rajbir	ਰਾਜਬੀਰ	Hero of Kingdom
Rajvansh	ਰਾਜਵੰਸ਼	Family of the king
Rajesh	ਰਾਜੇਸ਼	Supreme king
Rajni	ਰਜਨੀ	Night
Rajneesh	ਰਜਨੀਸ਼	Moon
Rajdev	ਰਾਜਦੇਵ	God king
Raman	ਰਮਨ	Pleasing, beloved, Merriment
Ramanpreet	ਰਮਨਪ੍ਰੀਤ	Love of beloved, love of Merriment
Ramanjit	ਰਮਨਜੀਤ	Victory of beloved
Ramandeep	ਰਮਨਦੀਪ	Light of beloved
Raminder	ਰਮਿੰਦਰ	Beloved God
Ramneet	ਰਮਨੀਤ	Engrossed in beloved
Ramnik	ਰਮਣੀਕ	Beautiful, charming
Ranbir	ਰਣਬੀਰ	Hero of battle

ੴ

Randeep	ਰਣਦੀਪ	Light of battle
Ranjit	ਰਣਜੀਤ	Victorious in battle
Ratan	ਰਤਨ	Gem
Rattanjot	ਰਤਨਜੋਤ	Flame of gem
Rattandeep	ਰਤਨਦੀਪ	Lamp of gem
Ravideep	ਰਵੀਦੀਪ	Light of Sun
Ravinder	ਰਵਿੰਦਰ	Lord Sun
Ravijeet	ਰਵਿਜੀਤ	Victory of sun
Rashmi	ਰਸ਼ਮੀ	Ray
Rajwant	ਰਾਜਵੰਤ	King
Ranjodh	ਰਣਜੋਧ	Warrior in battle
Ranpreet	ਰਣਪ੍ਰੀਤ	Love of battle
Randeep	ਰਣਦੀਪ	Light of battle
Ranjeev	ਰਣਜੀਵ	Life of battle
Rachna	ਰਚਨਾ	Creation
Randhir	ਰਣਧੀਰ	Resolute in battle
Raghubir	ਰਘੁਬੀਰ	Hero of Raghu family, Lord Rama
Ragini	ਰਾਗਿਨੀ	Musical notes

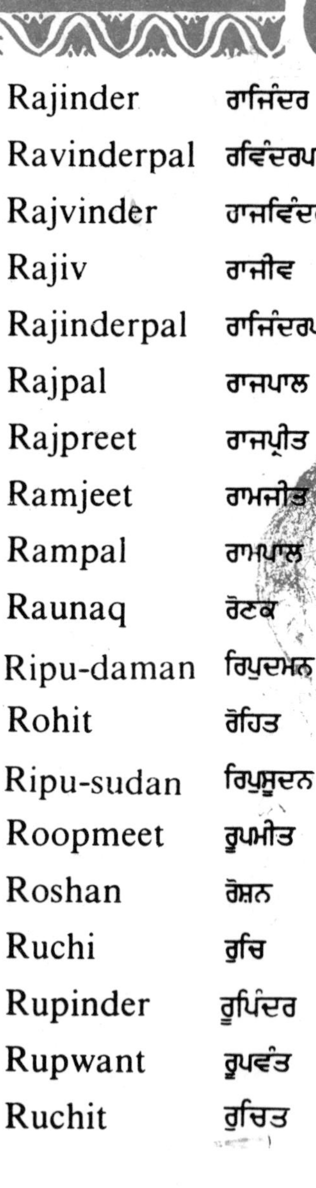

Rajinder	ਰਾਜਿੰਦਰ	Lord of king
Ravinderpal	ਰਵਿੰਦਰਪਾਲ	Protected by lord Sun
Rajvinder	ਰਾਜਵਿੰਦਰ	Great king
Rajiv	ਰਾਜੀਵ	Lotus
Rajinderpal	ਰਾਜਿੰਦਰਪਾਲ	Protected by lord king
Rajpal	ਰਾਜਪਾਲ	Protected by the king
Rajpreet	ਰਾਜਪ੍ਰੀਤ	Love of king
Ramjeet	ਰਾਮਜੀਤ	Victory of God.
Rampal	ਰਾਮਪਾਲ	Protected by God
Raunaq	ਰੌਣਕ	Gaiety
Ripu-daman	ਰਿਪੁਦਮਨ	Destroyer of enemy
Rohit	ਰੋਹਿਤ	Red, Blood
Ripu-sudan	ਰਿਪੁਸੂਦਨ	Destroyer of enemy
Roopmeet	ਰੂਪਮੀਤ	Friend of beauty
Roshan	ਰੋਸ਼ਨ	Lighted
Ruchi	ਰੁਚਿ	Interest
Rupinder	ਰੁਪਿੰਦਰ	Lord of beauty
Rupwant	ਰੂਪਵੰਤ	Full of beauty
Ruchit	ਰੁਚਿਤ	Bright, liked, Interested

ੴ

S ਸ

Sahaj	ਸਹਿਜ	Natural
Sahiba	ਸਾਹਿਬਾ	The Lady
Sahib	ਸਾਹਿਬ	The Master
Sajjan	ਸਜੱਣ	Virtuous Man
Smriti	ਸਮ੍ਰਿਤੀ	Remembrance
Sandeep	ਸੰਦੀਪ	Beautiful
Sanjog	ਸੰਜੋਗ	Chance, cohesion
Sadhna	ਸਾਧਨਾ	Devotion
Sarvottam	ਸਰਵੋਤੱਮ	The best
Swaranjeet	ਸਵਰਨਜੀਤ	Gold winner
Sawinder	ਸਵਿੰਦਰ	Beautiful God
Sawan	ਸਾਵਣ	Rainy month in vikram, calender
Sartaj	ਸਰਤਾਜ	Supreme master
Sangita	ਸੰਗੀਤਾ	Musical
Sanjana	ਸੰਜਨਾ	Gentle

ੴ

Satya	ਸਤਿਆ	Truth
Sartaj	ਸਰਤਾਜ	Crown
Saroj	ਸਰੋਜ	Lotus
Sanman	ਸਨਮਾਨ	Honour
Sansar	ਸੰਸਾਰ	The World
Sangat	ਸੰਗਤ	Company
Sangatjeet	ਸੰਗਤਜੀਤ	Victory of good company
Sangeet	ਸੰਗੀਤ	Music
Sachdev	ਸਚਦੇਵ	God of truth
Sachpreet	ਸਚਪ੍ਰੀਤ	Love for Truth
Sanjeevan	ਸੰਜੀਵਨ	Good life
Santsev	ਸੰਤਸੇਵ	Service of saints
Santjeet	ਸੰਤਜੀਤ	Victory for saints
Santprakash	ਸੰਤਪ੍ਰਕਾਸ਼	Light of saints
Satsangat	ਸਤਿਸੰਗਤ	Good company
Satsev	ਸਤਿਸੇਵ	Truthful service
Satkirat	ਸਤਿਕੀਰਤ	Truthful Fame
Satinder	ਸਤਿੰਦਰ	God of Truth
Satinderjeet	ਸਤਿੰਦਰਜੀਤ	Victory for the God of truth

ੴ

Satinderpal	ਸਤਿੰਦਰਪਾਲ	Protected by the God of truth
Satnam	ਸਤਿਨਾਮ	True name
Satbir	ਸਤਿਬੀਰ	True brave
Satwant	ਸਤਵੰਤ	Full of truth
Satvinder	ਸਤਿਵਿੰਦਰ	God of truth
Santokh	ਸੰਤੋਖ	Satisfaction, Contentment
Sadeev	ਸਦੀਵ	Permanent
Samrath	ਸਮਰੱਥ	Capable, powerful
Sameer	ਸਮੀਰ	Air, Breeze
Sarjeet	ਸਰਜੀਤ	Victorious
Sarabjeet	ਸਰਬਜੀਤ	All victorious
Sarabdayal	ਸਰਬਦਿਆਲ	Mercy for all
Sarabdev	ਸਰਬਦੇਵ	All pervading God
Sarabnidhan	ਸਰਬਨਿਧਾਨ	All treasure
Sarabpal	ਸਰਬਪਾਲ	Protector of all
Sarabpreet	ਸਰਬਪ੍ਰੀਤ	Love for all
Swaraj	ਸਵਰਾਜ	Own rule
Sadanand	ਸਦਾਨੰਦ	Eternal bliss

Sadeepan	ਸੰਦੀਪਨ	Lighted up
Sadgati	ਸਦਗਤੀ	Emancipation
Sagar	ਸਾਗਰ	Ocean
Sahdev	ਸਹਦੇਵ	God companion
Savitoj	ਸਵਿਤੋਜ	Splendour of sun
Samar	ਸਮਰ	War
Samarjeet	ਸਮਰਜੀਤ	Victor in war
Samarpal	ਸਮਰਪਾਲ	Fostered in war
Samarpreet	ਸਮਰਪ੍ਰੀਤ	Love for war
Samarinder	ਸਮਰਿੰਦਰ	God of war
Samata	ਸਮਤਾ	Equality
Sampat	ਸੰਪਤ	Prosperity
Sanjay	ਸੰਜੈ	Attached
Saral	ਸਰਲ	Straight, simple
Sarla	ਸਰਲਾ	Straight, honest
Sarabdaman	ਸਰਬਦਮਨ	Destroyer of all
Satish	ਸਤੀਸ਼	Lord Shiva
Satyajeet	ਸਤਿਆਜੀਤ	Victory for truth
Satmohan	ਸਤਿਮੋਹਨ	True attraction

ੴ

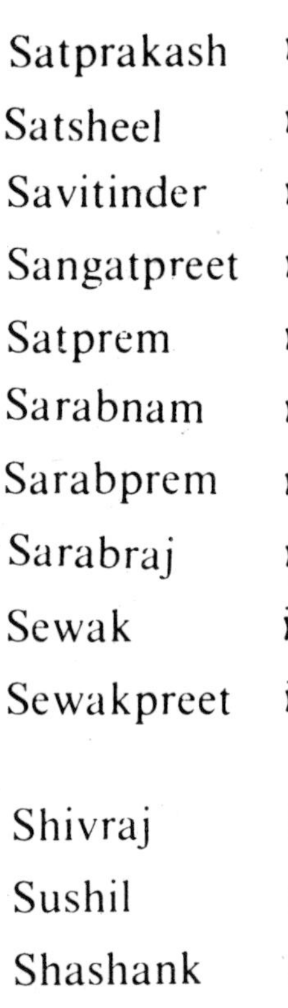

Satprakash	ਸਤਿਪ੍ਰਕਾਸ਼	Light of truth
Satsheel	ਸਤਿਸ਼ੀਲ	Truthful
Savitinder	ਸਵਿਤਿੰਦਰ	The Sun
Sangatpreet	ਸੰਗਤਪ੍ਰੀਤ	who loves the good company
Satprem	ਸਤਿਪ੍ਰੇਮ	Love for truth, True love
Sarabnam	ਸਰਬਨਾਮ	All pervading name of God
Sarabprem	ਸਰਬਪ੍ਰੇਮ	Who loves all
Sarabraj	ਸਰਬਰਾਜ	Great king
Sewak	ਸੇਵਕ	One who serves
Sewakpreet	ਸੇਵਕਪ੍ਰੀਤ	One who loves Servants of God
Shivraj	ਸ਼ਿਵਰਾਜ	God King, Lord shiva
Sushil	ਸੁਸ਼ੀਲ	Good character
Shashank	ਸ਼ਸ਼ਾਂਕ	The Moon
Shikha	ਸ਼ਿਖਾ	A pointed flame
Shyam	ਸ਼ਿਆਮ	Black, Lord Krishna
Shivdev	ਸ਼ਿਵਦੇਵ	Lord shiva
Sheelwant	ਸ਼ੀਲਵੰਤ	Full of modesty
Sardul	ਸਰਦੂਲ	Lion

ੴ

Sheetal	ਸ਼ੀਤਲ	Pleasing, cold
Sharan	ਸ਼ਰਨ	shelter (of God)
Sharanjeet	ਸ਼ਰਨਜੀਤ	Victory for the shelter under God
Sharanpal	ਸ਼ਰਨਪਾਲ	Protected by the shelter of God
Shubhpreet	ਸ਼ੁਭਪ੍ਰੀਤ	Auspicious love
Shobha	ਸ਼ੋਭਾ	Grace, Elegance
Shobhawant	ਸ਼ੋਭਾਵੰਤ	Fuul of grace
Shailinder	ਸ਼ੈਲਿੰਦਰ	King of mountains, Lord Shiva
Shatrujeet	ਸ਼ਤਰੂਜੀਤ	Victorious over enemies
Sharmila	ਸ਼ਰਮੀਲਾ	Happy
Shefali	ਸ਼ੇਫ਼ਾਲੀ	A flower
Shekhar	ਸ਼ੇਖਰ	Top, Peak, Crest, An excellent
Shishupal	ਸ਼ਿਸ਼ੂਪਾਲ	Protector of babies
Shishupreet	ਸ਼ਿਸ਼ੂਪ੍ਰੀਤ	Lover of babies
Shivender	ਸ਼ਿਵੇਂਦਰ	God, Lord Shiva
Shardha	ਸ਼ਰਧਾ	veneration
Shrikirti	ਸ਼ਿਰੀਕੀਰਤੀ	Lustrous, fame

ੴ

Shamsher	ਸ਼ਮਸ਼ੇਰ	Brave
Shaminder	ਸ਼ਮਿੰਦਰ	Quite, gentle
Simran	ਸਿਮਰਨ	Recollection, remembrance
Simranjeet	ਸਿਮਰਨਜੀਤ	Victory for remembrance
Simranpreet	ਸਿਮਰਨਪ੍ਰੀਤ	Love for remembrance
Simranpal	ਸਿਮਰਨਪਾਲ	Protected by remembrance
Sidharth	ਸਿੱਧਾਰਥ	Lord Budha
Sirjan	ਸਿਰਜਨ	Creation
Sohan	ਸੋਹਨ	Beautiful
Sohinder	ਸੋਹਿੰਦਰ	God of beauty
Sumeet	ਸੁਮੀਤ	Good friend
Supreet	ਸੁਪ੍ਰੀਤ	Good love
Sunder Saroop	ਸੁੰਦਰ ਸਰੂਪ	Beautiful shape
Sugeet	ਸੁਗੀਤ	Good song
Sukhjinder	ਸੁਖਜਿੰਦਰ	God of happiness
Sukhanand	ਸੁਖਾਨੰਦ	Pleasure, Bliss
Sukhinder	ਸੁਖਇੰਦਰ	God of happiness
Sukhjeet	ਸੁਖਜੀਤ	Victorious in happiness
Sukhdev	ਸੁਖਦੇਵ	God of happiness

ੴ

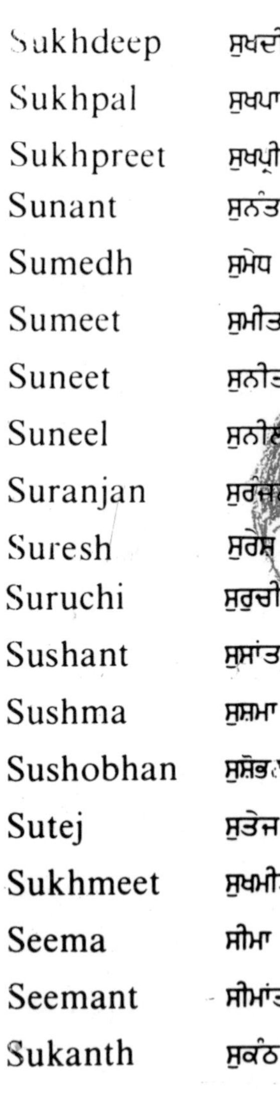

Sukhdeep	ਸੁਖਦੀਪ	Light of happiness
Sukhpal	ਸੁਖਪਾਲ	Protected by happiness
Sukhpreet	ਸੁਖਪ੍ਰੀਤ	Love for happiness
Sunant	ਸੁਨੰਤ	Attentive
Sumedh	ਸੁਮੇਧ	Wise
Sumeet	ਸੁਮੀਤ	Good friend
Suneet	ਸੁਨੀਤ	Good principles, Prudent
Suneel	ਸੁਨੀਲ	Blue
Suranjan	ਸੁਰੰਜਨ	Very pleasing
Suresh	ਸੁਰੇਸ਼	God Lord Indra
Suruchi	ਸੁਰੁਚੀ	Good taste
Sushant	ਸੁਸਾਂਤ	Quite peaceful
Sushma	ਸੁਸ਼ਮਾ	Beauty
Sushobhan	ਸੁਸ਼ੋਭਨ	Very beautiful
Sutej	ਸੁਤੇਜ	Lustre
Sukhmeet	ਸੁਖਮੀਤ	A friend who gives happiness
Seema	ਸੀਮਾ	Range Limit
Seemant	ਸੀਮਾਂਤ	Limit, Margin
Sukanth	ਸੁਕੰਠ	Sweet voiced

ੴ

Sukirat	ਸੁਕੀਰਤ	Reputation
Sukumar	ਸੁਕੁਮਾਰ	Delicate
Sukrit	ਸੁਕ੍ਰਿਤ	good deeds
Sukriti	ਸੁਕ੍ਰਿਤੀ	Virtuous
Sudhanshu	ਸੁਧਾਂਸ਼ੁ	The moon
Sunam	ਸੁਨਾਮ	Repute, good will
Subodh	ਸੁਬੋਧ	Intelligible, Easy
Suman	ਸੁਮਨ	A flower, Happy
Suruchi	ਸੁਰੁਚਿ	Good taste
Sulakhan	ਸੁਲੱਖਣ	Gifted with laudable ways
Sukhbir	ਸੁਖਬੀਰ	Happy brave
Sukhraj	ਸੁਖਰਾਜ	King of happiness
Sukhbans	ਸੁਖਬੰਸ	Happy family
Sukhwant	ਸੁਖਵੰਤ	Full of happiness
Sujan	ਸੁਜਾਨ	Learned, Wise, Intellingent,
Sunder	ਸੁੰਦਰ	Beautiful
Sunderjeet	ਸੁੰਦਰਜੀਤ	Victory for beauty
Sudarshan	ਸੁਦਰਸ਼ਨ	Good appearance, Beautiful
Suhas	ਸੁਹਾਸ	Beautiful smile

ੴ

Sudesh	ਸੁਦੇਸ਼	Good country
Sudha	ਸੁਧਾ	Nectar
Suneet	ਸੁਨੀਤ	Well behaved
Suchet	ਸੁਚੇਤ	Conscious
Surjit	ਸੁਰਜੀਤ	Victory of God
Surchet	ਸੁਰਚੇਤ	God consciousness
Surjan	ਸੁਰਜਨ	Godly people
Surjanmeet	ਸੁਰਜਨਮੀਤ	Friend of godly people
Surjot	ਸੁਰਜੋਤ	God's flame
Surpal	ਸੁਰਪਾਲ	Protected by God
Surinder	ਸੁਰਿੰਦਰ	The chief of gods
Surinderjeet	ਸੁਰਿੰਦਰਜੀਤ	Victory of God
Surinderpal	ਸੁਰਿੰਦਰਪਾਲ	Protected by God
Suraj	ਸੁਰਾਜ	Good rule
Sudhakar	ਸੁਧਾਕਰ	The moon
Sudeep	ਸੁਦੀਪ	Bright
Sudhir	ਸੁਧੀਰ	Calm
Suhirday	ਸੁਹਿਰਦੇ	Good hearted
Sujeet	ਸੁਜੀਤ	Winner

ੴ

Sukant	ਸੁਕਾਂਤ	Handsome
Sukesh	ਸੁਕੇਸ਼	With beautiful hair
Sulochan	ਸੁਲੋਚਨ	With beautiful eyes
Sumant	ਸੁਮੰਤ	Wise

T ਟ

Tarun	ਤਰੁਨ	Young
Tarunpal	ਤਰੁਨਪਾਲ	Protecter by Youthfulness
Taran	ਤਾਰਨ	Freedom from bondage, redemption,Salvation,
Taranjit	ਤਾਰਨਜੀਤ	Victory over bondage
Taranpreet	ਤਾਰਨਪ੍ਰੀਤ	Love for freedom from bondage
Tapinder	ਤਪਿੰਦਰ	God of devotion
Tavleen	ਤਵਲੀਨ	Absorbed in God
Teghbir	ਤੇਗਬੀਰ	Brave
Tejwant	ਤੇਜਵੰਤ	Full of splendour
Tejinder	ਤੇਜਿੰਦਰ	God of splendour
Tejdeep	ਤੇਜਦੀਪ	Light of splendour
Tejpratap	ਤੇਜਪ੍ਰਤਾਪ	Glory and splendour

ੳ

Tejpal	ਤੇਜਪਾਲ	Protecter of splendour
Tejbhan	ਤੇਜਭਾਨ	Sun of splendour
Tejbir	ਤੇਜਬੀਰ	Brave with splendour
Thakur	ਠਾਕੁਰ	Master, God
Tirath	ਤੀਰਥ	Sacred place
Trilochan	ਤਰਲੋਚਨ	Lord Shiva
Trilok	ਤਰਲੋਕ/ਤ੍ਰਿਲੋਕ	Three worlds
Trikal	ਤ੍ਰਿਕਾਲ	Three times
Tripat	ਤ੍ਰਿਪਤ	Satisfied
Tripal	ਤ੍ਰਿਪਾਲ	Protector of three worlds
Tribhuwan	ਤ੍ਰਿਭਵਨ	Three worlds

U ੳ

Uchit	ਉਚਿਤ	Proper, Right
Uchitpal	ਉਚਿਤਪਾਲ	Protector of right
Uchpal	ਉਚਪਾਲ	Protector of elevation
Uchpreet	ਉਚਪ੍ਰੀਤ	Love of elevation

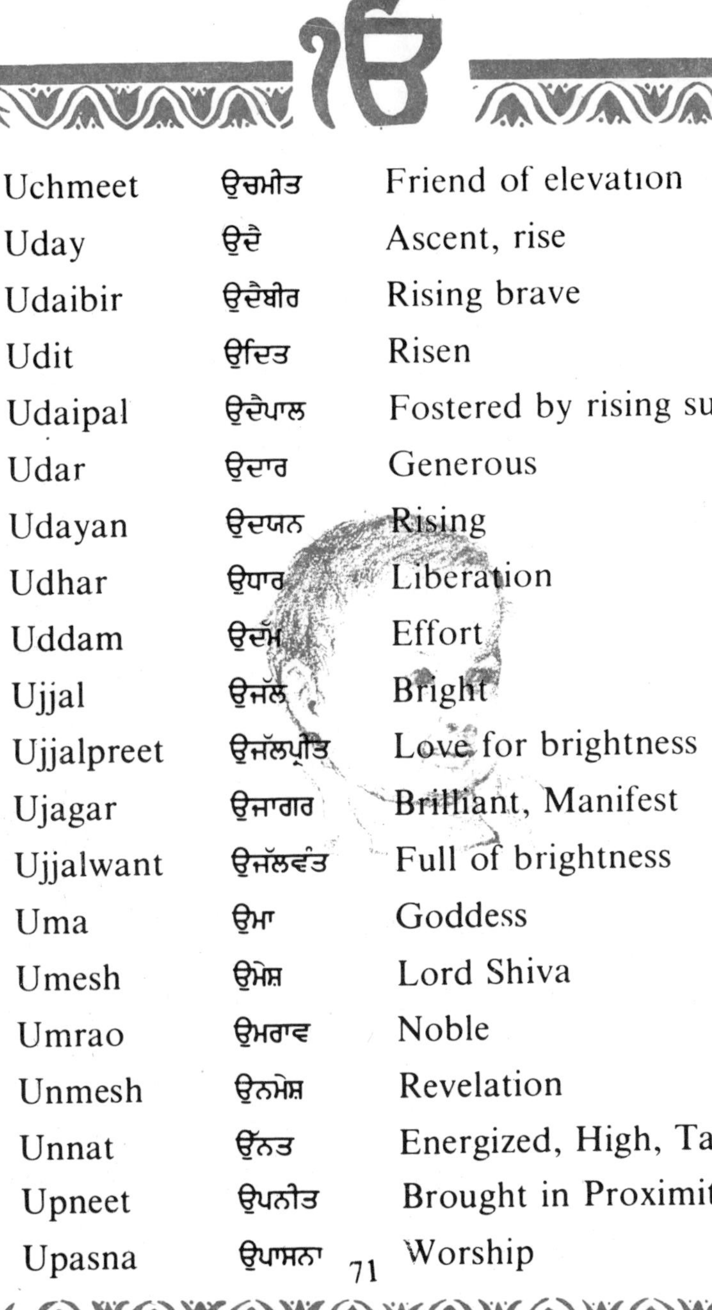

Uchmeet	ਉਚਮੀਤ	Friend of elevation
Uday	ਉਦੈ	Ascent, rise
Udaibir	ਉਦੈਬੀਰ	Rising brave
Udit	ਉਦਿਤ	Risen
Udaipal	ਉਦੈਪਾਲ	Fostered by rising sun
Udar	ਉਦਾਰ	Generous
Udayan	ਉਦਯਨ	Rising
Udhar	ਉਧਾਰ	Liberation
Uddam	ਉਦੱਮ	Effort
Ujjal	ਉਜੱਲ	Bright
Ujjalpreet	ਉਜੱਲਪ੍ਰੀਤ	Love for brightness
Ujagar	ਉਜਾਗਰ	Brilliant, Manifest
Ujjalwant	ਉਜੱਲਵੰਤ	Full of brightness
Uma	ਉਮਾ	Goddess
Umesh	ਉਮੇਸ਼	Lord Shiva
Umrao	ਉਮਰਾਵ	Noble
Unmesh	ਉਨਮੇਸ਼	Revelation
Unnat	ਉੱਨਤ	Energized, High, Tall
Upneet	ਉਪਨੀਤ	Brought in Proximity
Upasna	ਉਪਾਸਨਾ	Worship

ੴ

Upender	ਉਪਿੰਦਰ	Proximity of God
Upkar	ਉਪਕਾਰ	Benificence
Upjeet	ਉਪਜੀਤ	Victory for proximity
Upraj	ਉਪਰਾਜ	King of Proximity
Upma	ਉਪਮਾ	Simile, Praise
Urmil	ਉਰਮਿਲ	Full of waves
Usha	ਉਸ਼ਾ	Dawn
Ushakant	ਉਸ਼ਾਕਾਂਤ	The Sun
Ushakiran	ਉਸ਼ਾਕਿਰਣ	The first rays
Uttam	ਉਤੱਮ	Best
Uttamjeet	ਉਤੱਮਜੀਤ	Victory of the best
Uttamdeep	ਉਤੱਮਦੀਪ	Light of the best
Uttamjot	ਉਤੱਮਜੋਤ	Flame of the best
Uttammeet	ਉਤੱਮਮੀਤ	Friend of the best
Uttampreet	ਉਤੱਮਪ੍ਰੀਤ	Love of the best
Utkarsh	ਉਤਕਰਸ਼	Advancement
Utpal	ਉਤਪਲ	Lotus
Uttar	ਉਤਰ	North, Answer, After
Utsav	ਉਤਸਵ	Celebration

ੴ

V ਵ

Varun	ਵਰੁਨ	Deity of waters, God
Varunjeet	ਵਰੁਨਜੀਤ	Victory of God
Varundeep	ਵਰੁਨਦੀਪ	Lamp of God
Vandit	ਵੰਦਿਤ	Revered
Varunpal	ਵਰੁਨਪਾਲ	Protected by God
Vandan	ਵੰਦਨ	Adoration
Vasant	ਵਸੰਤ	Spring
Vachan	ਵਚਨ	Word
Variyam	ਵਰਿਆਮ	Lion
Vaibhav	ਵੈਭਵ	Riches
Vallabh	ਵਲੱਭ	Beloved
Vanjeet	ਵਨਜੀਤ	Lord of the forest
Vani	ਵਾਣੀ	Sayings
Varinder	ਵਰਿੰਦਰ	Lord of ocean
Varsha	ਵਰਸ਼ਾ	Rain
Vasudev	ਵਾਸੁਦੇਵ	Father of Lord Krishna
Vasudha	ਵਸੁਧਾ	The earth

ੴ

Vatsal	ਵਤਸਲ	Affectionate
Vibhakar	ਵਿਭਾਕਰ	The Moon
Ved	ਵੇਦ	A Sacred text The Vedas
Ved Prakash	ਵੇਦ-ਪ੍ਰਕਾਸ਼	Light of the vedas
Veena	ਵੀਨਾ	Flute
Vineet	ਵਿਨੀਤ	Modest
Vinay	ਵਿਨੈ	Modesty
Vinaydeep	ਵਿਨੈਦੀਪ	Lamp of modesty
Vinaybir	ਵਿਨੈਬੀਰ	Brave of modesty
Vinaypreet	ਵਿਨੈਪ੍ਰੀਤ	Love for modesty
Vikram	ਵਿਕਰਮ	Bravery, Valour
Vikramjit	ਵਿਕਰਮਜੀਤ	Victory for bravery
Vikramdev	ਵਿਕਰਮਦੇਵ	God of valour
Vijay	ਵਿਜੈ	Victory
Vijaypratap	ਵਿਜੈਪ੍ਰਤਾਪ	Glory of victory
Vivek	ਵਿਵੇਕ	Wisdom
Vivekdeep	ਵਿਵੇਕਦੀਪ	Light of wisdom
Vivekpreet	ਵਿਵੇਕਪ੍ਰੀਤ	Love for wisdom

ੴ

Vishwajeet	ਵਿਸ਼ਵਜੀਤ	Victory of the world
Vishwanath	ਵਿਸ਼ਵਨਾਥ	Lord of the world
Vishwa-jot	ਵਿਸ਼ਵਜੋਤ	Light of the world
Vishwapal	ਵਿਸ਼ਵਪਾਲ	Protector of the world
Vishweshwar	ਵਿਸ਼ਵੇਸ਼ਵਰ	Lord of the world
Vishwesh	ਵਿਸ਼ਵੇਸ਼	The Lord, Almighty
Vishwas	ਵਿਸ਼ਵਾਸ	Trust
Virajesh	ਵਿਰਜੇਸ਼	Lord Krishna
Vishwarpreet	ਵਿਸ਼ਵਪ੍ਰੀਤ	Love of the world
Vishwabir	ਵਿਸ਼ਵਬੀਰ	Brave in the world
Vir	ਵੀਰ	Brave
Virpal	ਵੀਰਪਾਲ	Protector of the brave
Vibha	ਵਿਭਾ	Light
Vibhuti	ਵਿਭੂਤਿ	Great, Dignity, Glory, Goddess of wealth
Vidya	ਵਿਦਿਆ	Learning, Knowledge
Vidyasagar	ਵਿਦਿਆਸਾਗਰ	Ocean of learning
Vijeta	ਵਿਜੈਤਾ	Victorious
Vijender	ਵਿਜੇਂਦਰ	Victorious God

Vikas	ਵਿਕਾਸ	Development, Bloom, Evolution
Vikesh	ਵਿਕੇਸ਼	The moon
Vimal	ਵਿਮਲ	Pure
Vinesh	ਵਿਨੇਸ਼	Godly
Vinod	ਵਿਨੋਦ	Enterainment, Happiness
Vipin	ਵਿਪਿਨ	Forest
Viplav	ਵਿਪਲਵ	Revolution
Vipul	ਵਿਪੁਲ	Plenty
Viresh	ਵਿਰੇਸ਼	Brave lord
Vishal	ਵਿਸ਼ਾਲ	Immense, Tremendous, Enormous
Vishwaraj	ਵਿਸਵਰਾਜ	King of the world
Vishw-Atam	ਵਿਸ਼ਵਆਤਮ	Soul of the world